WHAT
EPISCOPALIANS
BELIEVE

WHAT EPISCOPALIANS BELIEVE

AN INTRODUCTION

SAMUEL WELLS

Morehouse Publishing
A division of Church Publishing Incorporated

Morehouse Publishing, 4775 Linglestown Road, Harrisburg, PA 17112

Morehouse Publishing, 445 Fifth Avenue, New York, NY 10016

Morehouse Publishing is an imprint of Church Publishing Incorporated.

www.churchpublishing.org

Cover design by Laurie Klein Westhafer

Typeset by Bottom Line Publishing Services

Library of Congress Cataloging-in-Publication Data

Wells, Samuel, 1965-
    What episcopalians believe : an introduction / Samuel Wells.
      p. cm.
    Includes bibliographical references.
    ISBN 978-0-8192-2310-4 (pbk.)
    1. Episcopal Church--Doctrines. I. Title.
BX5930.3.W45   2011
230'.3--dc22   2011017603

Printed in the United States of America

For John, Ana, Ray, Tony, Charlie, and Ann

TABLE OF CONTENTS

PREFACE

This book is written for anyone who wants to know more about the church they don't belong to, or wants to know more about the church they belong to but don't always understand. It is also for those who want to know why they should continue to be a part of the church, given that they've become all too aware of its imperfections and, perhaps, their own.

One challenging aspect of writing the book was what to call the members of the Episcopal Church.[1] Until recently, while "Episcopalians" was almost universal in the United States, "Anglicans" was the obvious name for referring to things held in common with all Christians in the worldwide Anglican Communion. However, "Anglican" has come to have a more complex set of associations. In recent years the term "Anglican" has been a way that groups in the United States, finding themselves in serious tension with the Episcopal Church, have nonetheless identified with the Anglican Communion as a whole, often by seeking oversight from a province in Africa or elsewhere. So there is a danger that in using the term "Anglican," I could be understood as speaking of doctrine or practice in distinction from that of the Episcopal Church, even though I have no such intention. It is also the case that there are many parts of the Anglican Communion—not just the United States—where members use the term Episcopalian rather than Anglican to refer to their church and their ecclesial identity. So, to be clear, when I use the term Episcopal (with a capital "E"), or "the Episcopal Church," I am always referring to American Episcopalians. Sometimes I use the term "Anglicans and Episcopalians" or "Episcopalians and Anglicans" when I want to emphasize that a belief or practice is almost universal across the Communion. When the term "Anglican" appears, it isn't intended to signal a nod to any particular party within current controversies in the United States or elsewhere, but to be a shorter and less cumbersome way of referring to the faith of the Anglican Communion as a whole.

1. While the official name of the church is The Episcopal Church (TEC), the title "the Episcopal Church" will be used throughout this book.

Duke Divinity School, though a United Methodist–affiliated institution, nonetheless has one of the strongest and most dynamic Episcopal and Anglican faculties to be found anywhere, and it is a profound honor to be a part of it. It is especially rewarding to think about one's own tradition in the presence of and in conversation with such a diverse and vibrant collection of voices from other traditions. I am grateful to members of the Anglican Episcopal House of Studies and its director, Jo Bailey Wells, for giving me opportunities to think through these issues in a classroom setting.

Several people read and commented on all or part of the manuscript. Bill Gregg offered a marvelous and absorbing engagement with the whole text, offering corrections, insights, and challenges, made all the more valuable by his dual vocation as a bishop of the Episcopal Church and a theologian. I have lost count of the ways his detailed and nuanced attention has improved my understanding and expression. Craig Uffman made a serious, scholarly, and wide-ranging response to the project, and changed my mind on several questions. John Inge gave a helpful reading as a bishop from a Church of England perspective. Lisa Fischbeck and Abby Kocher also read drafts and made suggestions with wisdom and grace. Meanwhile, Lauren Winner helped me understand American history more cogently. I am blessed to be able to draw on such colleagues and friends and to learn from them.

Rebekah Eklund has been a marvelous research assistant, finding and listing obscure sources, checking unusual details, correcting wayward manuscripts, patiently making thoughtful suggestions, and challenging overblown generalizations. She makes the burden of editing into a joy. My debt to her, in this and many other ventures, is beyond my calculation, and my gratitude is profound.

This book is dedicated to six people who have shown me faith, faithfulness, and friendship. The kingdom of heaven belongs to such as these.

INTRODUCTION

This is a book for the church. It is for that part of the church known as the Anglican Communion, and known in different places by local names, like the Church of England or the Episcopal Church. It is written, initially, for anyone who simply would like to know what a member of such a church would normally believe. Such a person may be approaching confirmation, and for the first time taking seriously the contours of an inherited faith. Or they may be coming from a different branch of the universal church—from Roman Catholicism, perhaps, or from nondenominational Protestantism, or from another Christian denomination—and wondering in what respects this church differs from the one they already know well. Or they may have grown up in another faith, or with no faith at all, and may now be more interested in what Christians in general believe, rather than the fine particulars of how they differ from one another.

This book is designed for each one of these possible circumstances. But it is also designed for those who frequently encounter people in such circumstances, including teachers of the faith in church, school, and college settings, clergy, seminary teachers, and all who are looking for a straightforward, brief, and accessible overview of Christianity from within the tradition of the Episcopal Church. I have therefore tried simply to articulate the Christian faith as seen in this broad tradition, and to offer an account that does justice to and may be welcomed by a wide range of perspectives.

We live in controversial times. That is no new or unique experience. Christians have always differed with one another about the theory and practice of their faith—and they always will. Various themes make these current times seem more critical than any before them: these include the rapid changes in what can be done through applied technology, the immense power of weaponry that could wipe out huge populations at a stroke, and the climatic challenge to the ecological balance that threatens the long-term well-being of all earthly life. There is always a crisis looming somewhere, and there will always be personalities who thrive on tension and interest groups that stand to benefit from portraying existing circumstances as potentially disastrous.

This book, by contrast, is not arguing that we live in especially momentous times. I believe that the key events in Christian history have already happened. These include the creation of the universe; the calling of and covenant with God's chosen people, the Jews; the incarnation, ministry, death, and resurrection of Jesus; and the sending of the Holy Spirit. The first chapter of the book is therefore given over to describing what these events are and what they mean. One day the whole story will come to an end. But in the meantime, no event can compare in significance to these decisive episodes in the story of salvation. Every generation faces the challenge of bringing these central events face-to-face with the pressing issues of the day, and responding to the questions of the day in ways that are faithful to the manner in which God has already been revealed. Indeed, one may go further and say that, in every generation, God gives the church opportunities to rediscover how abundant are the resources of the faith, and how vibrant are the gifts of the Holy Spirit for meeting what would otherwise seem daunting trials.

Just at this moment there are intense debates in the Anglican Communion about sexuality. Compared to the tectonic shifts in the planet and its biosphere, humankind's relation to creation, and the changes and damage human beings are capable of bringing upon one another, preoccupation with such issues may seem at best a displacement activity and at worst a willful distraction. Nonetheless, the debates are hard to ignore. Because there is so much concern about authority, I take time in the second chapter to consider it at some length. I don't doubt that the various approaches to current issues arise out of profound conviction, deep reflection, and long-percolated wisdom. Yet I do hope that those on different sides of the debates who consider it is time for parts of the church to "walk apart" will review the description of the faith offered in these pages, and wonder why, if we agree so substantially, it seems so necessary to part company. In short, if all parties can agree that this is their faith, can we not also see our need of one another?

It is often said that Episcopalians have no doctrine. That is not, of course, true. Such a statement is intended either to indicate that we base our understanding of God on those theological commitments established in the early, undivided era of the first five centuries of the church, and have seen no need to add to the doctrines inherited from such times; or to acknowledge that, unlike other Reformation traditions, such as Lutherans or Calvinists, we have not tended to identify ourselves with definitive doctrinal statements, but instead with the historic Apostles' and Nicene Creeds and with particular patterns of common prayer. This is indeed true, but it doesn't mean that

Episcopalians have no doctrine. The convention that the Episcopal Church is not doctrinal has encouraged us to direct disproportionate degrees of scholarly inquiry toward history: in studies of the Episcopal Church it is quite normal for the greater part of the work to be given over to history rather than doctrine. In this book I have tried to set a different course: I begin with doctrine, then secondly look to the sources of doctrine, and then thirdly proceed to the ways those doctrines are most visibly manifested; only coming to history fourthly, by way of conclusion. Perhaps the most significant Episcopalian method of perceiving doctrine is the context set in chapter three: it is not abstract, never simply a series of propositions, but stands always in relation to worship, ministry, and mission.

Episcopalians are sometimes teased for regarding themselves as particularly well-placed to participate in ecumenical dialogue, and being, like Israel, a people through whom others may find a blessing. The teasing is appropriate, for it is surely for others to identify traditions that are helpful in catalyzing the reunion of the churches, rather than for us to award the accolade to ourselves. Nonetheless, the word "and" appears close to the heart of the identity described in these pages, especially in the phrase "Catholic and Reformed." Not every Episcopalian (or, indeed, Anglican) agrees with the convergence identified in this phrase. But in general, the desire—which goes back to the English Queen Elizabeth I and the settlement of 1559—that the church should have a Catholic shape, with bishops, priests, and deacons, and sacraments of baptism and eucharist, while having a Protestant emphasis on the authority of Scripture and the preaching of the Word, remains one of the Anglican Communion's most deeply held commitments. We have no revered founder, no pivotal item of doctrine, no egregious error of another group of Christians against which we define ourselves, and no pivotal interpreter through whose definitive reading of Scripture all must be evaluated. There was never a crucial time when we have felt we could simply take up the New Testament and begin anew. Instead we have a tradition of common prayer, a general commitment to the well-being of all, including nonmembers of the church, and a desire to seek a faith that can be shared by people of a wide diversity of temperaments and backgrounds.

In these pages I make regular reference to three documents. Most often I refer to one or more of the forms of liturgy in use in the Anglican Communion, often known as the Book of Common Prayer. This is because Episcopalians and Anglicans are notable for the way their doctrine and ethics emerge from the crucible of corporate prayer. I also refer to one doctrinal statement, the Thirty-Nine Articles, as articulated by a convocation of the Church of England under Archbishop Matthew Parker in 1563 and included in the 1662 Book of Common Prayer. A revised version of these Articles was adopted by the Episcopal Church in the United States in 1801

and is included in the 1979 Book of Common Prayer. While this statement
does not have the authority of the historic creeds, and on matters of salvation and the church can be preoccupied, sometimes unhelpfully, with the
particular quarrels of the sixteenth century, it provides a helpful, though
not definitive, reference point for pursuing a Catholic-and-Reformed approach to doctrine. That is the spirit in which I quote it in this book. While
I grew up regarding this document as narrow and dated, and many continue to share this view, I have come to find it a fruitful conversation partner
and a significant foundation statement of Episcopal belief. The third document on which I draw is the Chicago-Lambeth Quadrilateral, which arose
in the late nineteenth century as a proposal for the reunion of the Roman
Catholic and Orthodox churches around four principles: the Old and New
Testaments, the Nicene and Apostles' Creeds, the sacraments of baptism
and eucharist, and the historic episcopate, locally adapted.

By what authority do I claim to be able to speak for a whole branch of
the worldwide church? None. I perhaps aim to speak *to* it, more than *for*
it. My words, particularly in chapter one, are more prescription than description: I recognize that my account goes beyond the latter. I describe
the faith to which I trust all Christians in the Anglican Communion subscribe, but I know the reality is much more diverse than the way I present
it. For most of that diversity I give genuine thanks. My attempt to represent the breadth of the church is to be found not so much in the first
three chapters, but more in the final one, which is specifically designed to
be descriptive. Chapter four, in short, bears testimony to the complica-
tions that arise when trying to live the first three chapters.

One final underlying aim of this work is to assist American and English Anglicans and Episcopalians in understanding one another. The
first three chapters outline the way our doctrine is shared. The fourth
chapter describes how our respective histories and contexts are different. It brings out contrasts between the established Church of England
and the nonestablished Episcopal Church, and between the varieties of
contexts that characterize the churches of the Anglican Communion. If
bonds of affection between our provinces are to be sustained, affirmed,
fostered, and deepened, members of our churches need to appreciate,
at least in outline, the different pressures and tensions and assumptions
and narratives within which we are each working.

And this goal, of increasing interecclesial understanding, is also a
personal one. I was born in the Anglican Church of Canada, raised in
the Church of England, trained for ordination in the Scottish Episcopal
Church, and currently minister, in an interdenominational setting, as a
priest of the Episcopal Church in the United States. I have been enriched
by the contexts in which I have lived and served. I trust, and pray, that
these diverse contexts will long continue to enrich one another.

CHAPTER ONE

The Faith

Introduction: The Triune God

God is in Christ. This central statement of Christian belief crystal-izes a number of distinct, but related, convictions.

First, the historical figure Jesus of Nazareth, born in Bethlehem, living in Galilee, dying and rising in Jerusalem, embodies every-thing good, beautiful, and true that comes from the inmost being of God. Jesus is the centripetal goal to which all searches for truth must look, and Jesus is the centrifugal force from which all good-ness flows. If one wants to know who God is and what God is like and how God acts, Jesus is the touchstone of any answer.

Second, Christ is not just *from the heart of* God: Christ *is* God. Our notion of God is shaped, or reshaped, in the light of having seen God in Christ. God is the same God that is revealed in the Old Testament and known to the Jews—the one God. But God is also made known in Christ, and that is a different, but closely related, notion of God, which thenceforth governs all perceptions of God.

Third, it is not just that God *was* in Christ, when Jesus was walking around Galilee in the first-century. God *is* in Christ today. That not only indicates a conviction that Christ is risen from the dead, but, given that Christ returned whence he came, it suggests a third dimension of God that does not have a human body, but makes the risen Christ present in people and actions and events of God's choosing. Jesus spoke of God as one with whom he had an intimate, familial, unbreakable bond: he used the language of father and son. But he also spoke of there being a regular, perpetual presence of God among his followers after he had returned to his Father. This presence was one of comfort, counsel, and advocacy, whom we call the Holy Spirit.

Thus God came to be known as Father, Son, and Holy Spirit. This is a relationship of three "persons," distinct from one another, yet in one "substance"—sharing one being. They are equal with one another, yet each has different roles; even in these different roles, however, the whole of God is present in each one. The first of the Thirty-Nine Articles states that "there is but one living and true God, everlasting, without body, parts, or passions; of infinite power, wisdom, and goodness; the Maker, and Preserver of all things both visible and invisible. And in unity of this Godhead there be three Persons, of one substance, power, and eternity; the Father, the Son, and the Holy Ghost."[1]

Concerns have been raised in recent years that this language is unhelpfully male. It can be (and has been) wrongly invoked to affirm patriarchal models of human relationships. There is no doctrinal justification for associating gender with God. Jesus' own usage, however, argues for retaining the traditional vocabulary, and as yet no alternative has emerged that retains both the personal and the interdependent dimensions of the Trinity. So this most central element of Christian belief, the name of the triune God, remains an unresolved area.

Transformation in Christ

The heart of the Christian faith is that God came among human beings as Jesus of Nazareth. Jesus is God, fully present to humanity, and humanity, fully present to God. Jesus expressed the full possibility of being human, and made known the full reality of God. The coming of God in Jesus broke down the dividing wall between God and humanity, and the false separation between one human being and another—and, indeed, the whole creation. This coming is the central moment in history: everything before it was a preparation for it, and everything since has taken place in the light of it. This transformation may be perceived in four dimensions, as follows.

First, it is perceived in Jesus' incarnation and birth. Jesus "was made man," in the words of the Nicene Creed; in the words of John 1:14, "The Word became flesh and lived among us." This means Jesus was fully

---

1. The Thirty-Nine Articles, or "Articles of Religion," are found in the Book of Common Prayer, 867–76. (Hereafter known as BCP.)

human, fully divine, and yet was one person. The Chalcedonian Creed of 451, which expresses most explicitly the union of Jesus' human and divine nature, states that Jesus is "to be acknowledged in two natures, inconfusedly, unchangeably, indivisibly, inseparably; the distinction of natures being by no means taken away by the union, but rather the property of each nature being preserved, and concurring in one Person and one Subsistence, not parted or divided into two persons, but one and the same Son."[2] In other words Jesus was and is a single person: but in that single person lies both a divine and a human nature, which are not blended but remain distinct.

One important way in which this conviction is expressed is in the doctrine of the virgin birth, which maintains that Jesus was born of a union between the Virgin Mary and the Holy Spirit, and that neither Joseph nor any other man was involved in Jesus' conception. Hence the Chalcedonian Creed states that Jesus was "begotten before all ages of the Father according to the Godhead, and in these latter days, for us and for our salvation, born of the Virgin Mary, the Mother of God, according to the Manhood." This doctrine emphasizes that salvation is entirely God's initiative. The term for "birth" in the original Greek of Matthew 1:18 is "genesis." This hints that the conception of Jesus—not specifically in Mary's womb, but God's decision never to be except to be for and with us in Christ—is the beginning of all creation, of all life, of all salvation, of everything that matters. Thus the creation itself was a kind of virgin birth, because it was creation from nothing, and it was brought about by the Holy Spirit. And the virgin birth was a new creation, or perhaps even the original creation, because it too was brought about in some ways out of nothing, by the action of the Holy Spirit.[3]

Another dimension of this belief in God's enfleshment in Christ is the delicate balance between the ways Jesus Christ is like humanity and the ways he is not. The Chalcedonian Creed states simply that Christ is "in all things like unto us, without sin." The second of the Thirty-Nine Articles adds, however, an extra assertion: that Jesus *truly suffered*. The Nicene Creed makes a similar claim when it recalls that Jesus "suffered under Pontius Pilate." If Jesus is to be regarded as fully God, he cannot sin, for God is "perfect in power, in love and purity," as the hymn puts it.[4] But if Jesus is to be regarded as fully human, he must suffer. The notion, known as "docetism," that Jesus only appeared to be human, and therefore could not experience human suffering, and thus only *seemed* to suffer on the cross, is a distortion of Christian doctrine that theologians

2. Found at http://www.creeds.net/ancient/chalcedon.htm.
3. For a more developed account of this argument, see Samuel Wells, *Speaking the Truth: Preaching in a Pluralistic Culture* (Nashville: Abingdon, 2008), 52–58.
4. Reginald Heber, "Holy, Holy, Holy, Lord God Almighty," *The Hymnal 1982*, 362.

have long sought to eradicate. Showing how Jesus entered wholly into human experience, yet was without sin, and exploring how Jesus suffered in a way that expressed, rather than took away from, the perfection of God, have been two projects close to the heart of Christology since the beginning.

As we shall see in chapter four, Jesus' incarnation has been a particular emphasis of Episcopal theology, particularly in the nineteenth and twentieth centuries.

Second, there is Jesus' ministry in Galilee. Despite constituting the majority of the narrative in all four gospels, this has never become the subject of controversy in the way other aspects of Jesus' life have. Thus, for example, the Nicene Creed omits his ministry altogether; and the Thirty-Nine Articles make no mention of it either—it is not even to be found in Article XXXV among the list of subjects of approved homilies. Yet such silence reflects consensus rather than neglect.

After Jesus was baptized by John and commissioned by the voice of the Father and the descent of the Holy Spirit, he faced a time of testing and temptation. Then he emerged to proclaim the reign of God and call disciples. The number of disciples—twelve, the same number as the tribes of Israel—reflected the way Jesus was reconstituting the people of God. This was also expressed in his ministry of teaching, in which, like Moses, he gave the people a way to live faithfully under God; and in his performance of miracles, enacted parables in which, like Elijah and Elisha, Jesus showed his oneness with God and his sovereignty over the human body and the forces that oppress it, such as sickness, hunger, and mighty storm. He also attracted controversy, and in his disputes with the religious and social authorities of his time, forthrightly proclaimed the righteousness of God that transcended their limited and self-serving perceptions. Thus Jesus *declared* the present and coming reign of God in his teaching, *demonstrated* it in his miracles, and *demanded* a response by calling people to follow him.

Third, there is the account of Jesus' passion and death. The gospels record that during his ministry in Galilee, Jesus turned toward Jerusalem, anticipating that his arrival there would presage his violent death. His challenge to the religious and social authorities of his day, demonstrated beyond question in his cleansing of the temple, and either implicit or explicit in his teaching and healing, provoked a plot to have him executed by the Romans. The crowds that had applauded his entrance into Jerusalem on a donkey turned against him days later and called for him to be crucified. Jesus died one of the most agonizing deaths imaginable, slowly asphyxiated while suspended by nails driven through his hands, all the while mocked and reviled by his persecutors and deserted by most of his disciples.

The death of Jesus is the focal moment of Christian devotion, in a way that transcends the precise historical circumstances that surround it. The crucifixion, it seems, is what happens when the profound and utter goodness of God comes face-to-face with the fickle and faithless machinations of humankind. The tremors resulting from the first tree, of Adam in the Garden of Eden, finally emerge in the second tree, of Jesus on Calvary. But somehow the horror of the cross lies deep in the purpose of God; hence the day of its commemoration is known as *Good* Friday. This goodness can be traced in two further Old Testament passages. One is the binding of Isaac in Genesis 22, where Abraham is called to give up his only son but is delivered when God sees his obedience and tells him to offer a ram instead. Jesus is seen as both the obedient son and the sacrificial ram, who dies in the place of others. The other passage is the servant songs of Isaiah 40–55, where Israel comes to see its vocation as suffering in order to reconcile God to the world, especially in Isaiah 53, where the language of being "led like a lamb to the slaughter" quickly became identified with Jesus' journey to the cross.

On a simply human level, Jesus did not *need* to go to the cross. He was an innocent man who could have found plenty of ways of avoiding the attentions of those who meant him harm. He made a free choice, just as hearers of his story ever since have made a free choice whether or not to recognize his suffering as God's gift to them. The poignancy of this free choice is most visible in his tortured prayer in the garden of Gethsemane: "My Father, if it is possible, let this cup pass from me; yet not what I want but what you want" (Matthew 26:39). His violent death was nonetheless almost inevitable, since, on a spiritual level, humanity seems incapable of tolerating profound goodness for very long, and, on a practical level, Jesus seems to have been unwilling or unable to cease his public ministry, which made him a perpetual source of exasperation to the authorities. Among many features of Jesus' suffering and death, the following have attracted particular attention:

- *Jesus' vicarious suffering as a sacrifice.* It is hinted at in the gospels (the term "ransom" in Mark 10:45, for example) and made much more explicit in Paul's letters that Jesus died for the sake of sinners—whether Israel, or all whom God has chosen, or all people, or all creation. Here lies the significance of Jesus' death coinciding with Passover, since the blood of the lamb signalled the angel of the Lord to pass over the houses of the Israelites in Exodus, and accordingly the blood of Jesus, the Lamb of God, causes God to pass over the people's sins. It's not clear precisely why Jesus' death causes God to "pass over" human sin, but the echo of the Passover lamb is frequently evident in the New Testament.

- *Jesus' nonresistance and forgiving demeanor as he went to his death.* The words, "He saved others; he cannot save himself" (Mark 15:31) and "Father, forgive them; for they do not know what they are doing" (Luke 23:34) perfectly express the irony and the pathos of Jesus' defenseless death. Jesus, in an extreme working-out of the logic of the incarnation, was handed over into the mercy of the merciless. Having started his life with his arms bound by a loving mother in swaddling clothes, he ended it with his arms nailed down by enemies on a cross: but still he loved his enemies as much as he loved his mother.

- *The isolation of Jesus, not just among human beings, but even, perhaps, in the heart of God.* Jesus' words from the cross, "My God, my God, why have you forsaken me?" have sometimes been interpreted as expressing the profound alienation of Jesus, even within the eternal and unbreakable mutual indwelling of the Holy Trinity. Whether this truly means there was a cross in the heart of God from the foundation of the world, or whether this is a grief and sorrow Jesus bore on behalf of sinners for a precise period of time, is not an easy question to resolve. (It could also be that, since Jesus is quoting Psalm 22, which ends positively, the words are actually a coded declaration of hope.) Regardless of the exact import of the words, they are a searing challenge to recognize the depth of human alienation from God, the extent of Jesus' identification with the human predicament, and the limitlessness of God's commitment to redeeming the world, even to the point of letting this alienation penetrate God's inner being.

The Thirty-Nine Articles insist, "As Christ died for us, and was buried, so also is it to be believed, that he went down into Hell" (Article III). This is noted in some versions of the Apostles' Creed, in the words "He descended into hell" (other versions say, "He descended to the dead"), but it is not mentioned in the Nicene Creed. The scriptural witness for this doctrine is slight, but the point is chiefly to address the complex issue of the salvation of those who had died before the coming of Christ. This suggestion, that Christ "harrowed" hell, a tradition in many places recalled in the liturgy of Holy Saturday, is a gesture toward resolving the anomalies that arise when salvation is restricted to those who believe, including the eternal status of those who, for a host of reasons, never had the chance to hear the gospel.

Fourth and last, there is the question of Jesus' resurrection and ascension. The resurrection of the incarnate Lord, Jesus Christ, is the focus of Christian faith, the historic beginning of Christian worship, and the foundation of Christian hope. This is because it represents—or achieves—God's sovereignty over sin and death, and shows that the conflict embodied on the cross is resolved forever. In the resurrection of Jesus, Christians see the promise of their own resurrection and the restoration of all creation.

A number of factors make the resurrection a complex doctrine. The gospel accounts do not narrate the resurrection itself in the way that they narrate Jesus' crucifixion and death. They simply describe Jesus' appearances to Mary and the disciples. The precise moment and manner of the resurrection remains veiled in mystery. Meanwhile, Jesus' resurrection appears to be a unique and unprecedented historical event, suspending conventional laws of nature and almost defying description. While Jesus is recorded as raising Lazarus (John 11:1–44) and the widow's son at Nain (Luke 7:11–15), his own resurrection is different because his bodily form, while still bearing the marks of the nails (John 20:25–27), is capable of sudden inexplicable appearances and disappearances (Luke 24:31–36). Some believers, while wishing to affirm God's sovereignty over sin and death, have found the notion of such a unique, bodily resurrection hard to endorse. It has been quite common in such circles to make a distinction between spiritual and bodily resurrection, with an approving nod to the former.

The Thirty-Nine Articles are unequivocal in their affirmation of Jesus' physical resurrection: "Christ did truly rise again from death, and took again his body, with flesh, bones, and all things appertaining to the perfection of Man's nature" (Article IV). This is not just recognition of scriptural authority. It indicates three further points. First, God's sovereignty over sin and death and his offer of forgiveness and everlasting life is the central point at stake, and every effort should be made to preserve faith in that sovereignty, rather than be waylaid by convictions about the physical universe. Second, it is vital that the resurrection demonstrates the completion of Christ's work on the cross. However precise the church's understanding of what was achieved on the cross, the resurrection is not simply an affirmation of it, but an integral part and completion of it. Third, the tendency to downplay the human body and to assert the primacy of the soul is a deep-seated strand in Christian theology and piety, going back to the Neoplatonic philosophy fashionable in the early centuries of the church; it contrasts with the very physical statement of faith that focuses on the incarnation of God in Christ. The logical implication of a nonphysical resurrection for Christ is, almost inevitably, the anticipation of a nonphysical hope of resurrection for Christians.

The relationship between the resurrection of Jesus Christ and the resurrection of all believers (or perhaps all people, or all things) is not a simple one. Without doubt, the resurrection of Jesus completes the work of the cross in restoring to the believer, through the forgiveness of sins, everything that has been lost in the past and, through the offer of everlasting life, everything that one might fear to lose in the future. The risen body of Jesus, bearing the marks of his passion yet with unprecedented powers, aptly portrays this double gift. But it gives no precise clue about what *form* the believer's risen body may take, nor *where* it may reappear (not in this life, like Jesus), nor *when*. Some have taken their cue from Jesus' words to the thief on the cross, "today you will be with me in Paradise" (Luke 23:43), and have seen them as a promise of immediate entry into heaven on the death of the believer. Others have taken the frequent references to "the last day" to indicate a general judgment for all creation, or all people, before which those who have died will remain in an unresolved state. Still others believe the words of Revelation 21 to be normative, and have perceived God as preparing a new heaven and a new earth that will transform all known forms of life, largely beyond recognition, thus rendering secondary our hopes for merely individual survival.

The key point about Jesus' ascension into heaven is not to speculate about whether heaven is "up there" and thus whether or not Jesus truly "went up." The point is, instead, that Jesus had completed his work among us. This is a point of struggle for many Christians, who may be inclined to feel, looking at the woes of the world, that there is a great deal left for him still to do. But it is essential to the faith to hold on to the conviction that Jesus has opened up the past through the forgiveness of sins and opened the future through the gift of eternal life, and any addition would be less, not more. The sending of the Holy Spirit and the final consummation on the last day are the logical fulfillment of Christ's coming, but they must not be described in such a way that might suggest Jesus' work in itself was anything less than complete. One negative consequence of losing a conviction that Christ's work is complete is the false notion that we must complete it ourselves. Our work must truly continue the trajectory of Christ's work, but any idea that we ourselves can save the world is bad for us and bad for the world, besides running contrary to the evidence of fragile and flawed human history.[5]

The People of God

Jesus was a Jew. Christians have repeatedly denied, or at least overlooked, this fact through the centuries. This deliberate or unintended ignorance has persisted despite the fact that the New Testament explores Jesus' Jewishness at length, particularly in Matthew's gospel, where Jesus is presented as the new Moses. The church's treatment of the Jews, particularly in its second millennium, constitutes one of its greatest failures.

5. This is clearly not the last word on mission. For further reflection, see chapter three, below.

To understand Jesus, one first needs to speak of Israel. There are four aspects of the term "Israel" that together play a significant role in providing a context and backdrop to the Christian faith.

First, Israel and covenant. Israel names the people to whom the character and purposes of God are disclosed, and through whom all the peoples of the earth are to find a blessing. The early chapters of Genesis tell of two paths God might have taken. One is to work with and through all humanity, represented by Adam and Eve; the other is to settle upon one righteous person, represented by Noah. Instead, God chose one people, beginning with Abraham, and the rest of Genesis shows how that people's identity emerges not through their own merit but through the grace of God. After Noah, God promised never again to destroy the earth (Genesis 9:11). This then becomes the dynamic that animates the whole Bible: how God will redeem humankind through a particular people without destroying the earth and in a way that blesses all peoples.

The defining experience of Israel lies in the Exodus. Largely narrated in the book of the same name in the Bible and the three that follow it, the Exodus refers to Israel's time of slavery in Egypt, the disclosure to Moses in the burning bush of both the identity of God and God's purpose to liberate the people, Israel's deliverance through God's miraculous hand, the giving of the covenant to Moses on Mount Sinai, and the entry into and conquest of the promised land under Joshua after forty years in the wilderness. This sequence of events became the touchstone for Israel's identity and the standard of Israel's faithfulness. For example, the prophets interpreted the oppression of landless and powerless people during the time of the kings as forgetfulness of who Israel truly was. As God had delivered Israel when Israel was in desperate straits, so the Israelites should show understanding and gratitude by treating the poor the way God had treated them.

The term that gathers together all these dimensions of Israel's experience is "covenant." Covenant also expresses the way various nations in Christian history have identified God's blessing to Israel and assigned it to themselves. Examples include the English in the nineteenth century, the Afrikaners in the twentieth century, and some in the United States today; in each of these groups, influential spokespersons have seen themselves as God's chosen people with a special mission.[6]

---

6. The theologian Oliver O'Donovan offers a more appropriate way to appreciate Israel's heritage faithfully. He speaks of God's reign, which brings together the decisive action of God in securing Israel's victory over enemies and in offering salvation. He next speaks of God's law, as the covenant made with Israel on Mt. Sinai and the ordering of life and exercise of judgment that it entailed. He then speaks of God's land, referring to the promised land as the visible token of God's provision. Finally he points to the people's response in praise. See Oliver O'Donovan, *The Desire of the Nations: Rediscovering the Roots of Political Theology* (Cambridge: Cambridge University Press, 1996), 30–49.

The second key element of Israel in the Christian faith is Israel's relationship to Jesus. God laments that the Sinai covenant has been broken, but resolves to remain Israel's parent (Hosea 11:1–11), and promises that there will be a new covenant, written on the hearts of the people (Jeremiah 31:31–35). Early Christians quickly identified that covenant with the one of which Jesus spoke at the Last Supper, and perceived the blood of Jesus as sealing the covenant, just as the blood of the lamb ensured that the angel of the Lord passed over the houses of the Hebrews on the eve of the Exodus. Furthermore, Jesus' ministry includes many gestures that imitate and revive dimensions of Israel's story. He calls twelve disciples, recalling the twelve tribes of Israel. He is baptized at the Jordan river, where Israel first came into the land. He goes up on a mountain like Moses to explain a code of ethics that improvises on the Sinai covenant, heals like the prophet Elijah, and goes down to Egypt like his forebears did. All the hopes of Israel converge on the person of Jesus.

Yet Christians continue to read not just the story of Jesus in the New Testament but also the story of Israel in the Old, and continue to call both testaments their Bible. The place of the Old Testament is thus the third dimension of Israel's place in the Christian imagination. Caricatures of the Old Testament persist. They include the view that the God of the Old Testament is a warrior, unlike the peaceable God of the New; that its usefulness resides simply in its prophecies of the coming Messiah; and that it is full of ritual and prohibition, whereas the New is full of grace and freedom. By contrast the Thirty-Nine Articles insist that the Old Testament is an indispensable part of the Bible, and that "both in the Old and New Testament everlasting life is offered to Mankind by Christ" (Article VII)—in other words that the gospel is to be discerned in the Old as well as in the New Testament. However, the Articles also maintain a longstanding tradition, first described in detail in the thirteenth century by Alexander of Hales and other Franciscan theologians, and adopted by Thomas Aquinas, that a distinction may be made between the ritual/ceremonial, the civil, and the moral commandments.[7] The moral commandments remain binding, even though with the new covenant the other commandments have ceased to be so (Article VII). Another subtle distinction concerns the place of the Apocrypha. The Articles include 1 and 2 Esdras among the canonical books and list a further fourteen books as ones to be read "for example of life and instruction of manners," but not as sources or grounds of doctrine (Article VI).

But what, then, of the Jews? This is the fourth aspect of the place of Israel in relation to Christianity. From the early centuries of the church,

---

7. The threefold division had been anticipated by the Jewish philosopher Maimonides. See Matthew Levering, *Christ's Fulfilment of Torah and Temple: Salvation according to Thomas Aquinas* (Notre Dame: University of Notre Dame Press, 2002), 6–8.

Christians have had a tendency to forget that Jesus was born of a Jewish mother and that the first disciples were Jews. They have often spoken as if all Jews bore responsibility for killing Jesus, highlighting the gospels' accounts of the raging mob rather than the first-century Jewish and Roman administrations in Jerusalem in particular; and they have tended to misunderstand, misrepresent, or even demonize postbiblical Judaism. The history of Christian relations with Judaism has been characterized by Christian inability to deal with Jewish difference, and by a catalogue of prejudices and misappropriated scriptural texts, sometimes exacerbated and manipulated for political advantage, frequently issuing in violent persecution, evolving in the nineteenth century into explicit anti-Semitism, and culminating in the Nazi Holocaust.

While there is widespread and almost universal repentance in the Anglican Communion today about this shameful history, the precise place of the Jews in the Christian view of the world and the church is still unclear. There is no consensus on whether Christians should, for example, still seek the conversion of Jews to Christianity. The status of God's promises to the Jews are not clear: while they still have a special and unshakeable place in God's heart, the incorporation of the Gentiles into God's people has clearly altered that relationship, but exactly how and to what extent is not certain. It seems these things are for God to know, and for the church to discover. Nor is it at all clear what should be the understanding of the secular contemporary state of Israel, the degree to which modern Israel should be associated with the identity and destiny of the Jewish people, and its rights and responsibilities in relation to its non-Jewish inhabitants and neighbors.

The Holy Spirit and the Church

How does the salvation offered in Christ take shape for human beings in history—most notably, for believers today? The answer to that question is the Holy Spirit. Article V of the Thirty-Nine Articles states, "The Holy Ghost, proceeding from the Father and the Son, is of one substance, majesty, and glory, with the Father and the Son, very and eternal God." This affirms that the Holy Spirit is an equal member of the Trinity, and thus fully God, but it remains reticent on the actual work of the Holy Spirit, which has been a tendency in Episcopal theology ever since. But the words of the Nicene Creed encourage further articulation: "I believe in the Holy Ghost, the Lord and Giver of Life; who proceeds from the Father and the Son; who with the Father and the Son together is worshiped and glorified; who spoke by the prophets." The sixth-century addition of the words "and the Son" is strongly disputed by the Eastern Orthodox churches, but the Episcopal tradition has sided with the western church, maintaining that only if the Spirit is understood as proceeding from both Father and Son is it possible to insist that all activities of the Spirit must resemble the God made known in Jesus. And that is the key to recognizing the work of the Spirit: it makes people and organizations and activities look like Jesus.

What the Holy Spirit does is to overcome the distance of space and time between Christ and the believer, and make Jesus present to the church today. For example, the risen and ascended Jesus sits at the right hand of the Father, but the Holy Spirit makes Jesus present in the elements of bread and wine in the service of Holy Communion. The Holy Spirit is also the giver of life: from hovering over the waters in Genesis 1 to giving the believer new birth (John 3:3–8) to healing the divisions of Babel portrayed in the tongues of fire on the day of Pentecost (Acts 2:1–4). This new life is fundamentally one that sets people free, as Jesus proclaims in the synagogue in Nazareth, "The Spirit of the Lord is upon me, because he has anointed me to bring good news to the poor. He has sent me to proclaim release to the captives and recovery of sight to the blind, to let the oppressed go free, to proclaim the year of the Lord's favor" (Luke 4:18–19). All of these works of the Spirit concern release from bondage. And the Spirit stands alongside believers as they withstand trials and temptations: Jesus says, "I will ask the Father, and he will give you another Advocate, to be with you forever. This is the Spirit of truth. . . . When the Advocate comes, whom I will send to you from the Father, the Spirit of truth who comes from the Father, he will testify on my behalf" (John 14:16–17; 15:26). The Spirit's advocacy will be at the most challenging times: "When they bring you to trial and hand you over, do not worry beforehand about what you are to say; but say whatever is given you at that time, for it is not you who speak, but the Holy Spirit" (Mark 13:11).

In the rite of baptism in the Episcopal Church, the Holy Spirit is named no less than six times in the prayer of thanksgiving over the water. The prayer describes many of the roles of the Spirit:

> We thank you, Almighty God, for the gift of water. Over it the Holy Spirit moved in the beginning of creation. . . . In it your Son Jesus received the baptism of John and was anointed by the Holy Spirit as the Messiah. . . . We thank you, Father, for the water of Baptism. . . . Through it we are reborn by the Holy Spirit. . . . We bring into [your Son's] fellowship those who come to him in faith, baptizing them in the Name of the Father, and of the Son, and of the Holy Spirit. Now sanctify this water, we pray you, by the power of your Holy Spirit. . . . To [Jesus Christ], to you, and to the Holy Spirit, be all honor and glory.[8]

---

8. BCP, 306–7.

But the Spirit is not just addressed to individuals. The church is that body of people in whom the Holy Spirit corporately dwells. The Spirit brings unity to that body. Just as the Spirit communicates the bondedness of the Trinity, so the Spirit draws together diverse communities and overcomes dividing walls of hostility. To do this the Spirit gives the church gifts. The purpose of these gifts, as Paul repeatedly stresses, is the building up of the body as a whole:

> To each is given the manifestation of the Spirit for the common good. To one is given through the Spirit the utterance of wisdom, and to another the utterance of knowledge according to the same Spirit, to another faith by the same Spirit, to another gifts of healing by the one Spirit, to another the working of miracles, to another prophecy, to another the discernment of spirits, to another various kinds of tongues, to another the interpretation of tongues. All these are activated by one and the same Spirit, who allots to each one individually just as the Spirit chooses. (1 Corinthians 12:7–11)

The emphasis in the Episcopal Church has generally been that the more dramatic gifts, such as speaking in tongues, are to take their place in the background, with the more abiding gifts such as faith, hope, and love in the foreground (1 Corinthians 13:1–3, 13). A community receiving the gifts of the Spirit in appropriately upbuilding ways may be expected to exhibit the fruits of the Spirit: "love, joy, peace, patience, kindness, generosity, faithfulness, gentleness, and self-control" (Galatians 5:22–23).

Part of the role of such gifts is to point the church's attention toward the climax of God's story in the *eschaton*, the "last day." The Spirit is described variously as a seal, or down payment, or guarantee of God's promises. For example, the Ephesians are told that they "were marked with the seal of the promised Holy Spirit; this is the pledge of our inheritance toward redemption as God's own people" (Ephesians 1:13–14). In the rite of baptism in the Episcopal Church, the priest or bishop makes a sin of the cross on the candidate's forehead, often using oil, and says, "You are sealed by the Holy Spirit in Baptism and marked as Christ's own for ever."[9] One further way this is expressed in worship is in the conclusion of the Great Thanksgiving at the eucharist. This third part of the prayer often dwells on the way the empowerment of the Spirit leads Christians to seek the Lord's consummation in actions advancing justice and peace, and to see the Spirit especially revealed among the oppressed of the earth—and increasingly in reference to the damaged soil, seas, and skies themselves.

The Thirty-Nine Articles describe the visible church as a congregation of the faithful "in which the pure Word of God is preached, and the

---

9. BCP, 308.

Sacraments. . . duly ministered according to Christ's ordinance" (Article XIX). The church and the Spirit are vitally interlinked, because it is above all the church that makes visible the possibilities of human interaction released by the saving work of Christ. Thus the church is the primary, though by no means only, sphere of the Spirit's activity. But if the church is to be, and to be seen as, both human and divine, like Christ, and not just a mundane and self-serving club or bureaucracy, the Spirit must infuse the structures of the church's life in personal, liberating, life-giving, unifying ways.

The Nicene Creed describes the church as "one, holy, catholic, and apostolic." Each of these words deserves attention, and highlights the work of the Spirit. The word "one" refers to the church's unity, which has always been a central concern of the Episcopal Church. Often Episcopalians describe themselves as both Catholic and Reformed. Sometimes, they perceive themselves as offering a *via media,* or "middle way," between Rome and Geneva (or even Rome and Constantinople). In these ways Episcopalians highlight their role and perhaps their calling as agents of unity not merely among diverse Christians in a single territory, but among Christians throughout the world. Jesus' words in his farewell discourses resonate strongly with Episcopalians:

> I ask not only on behalf of these, but also on behalf of those who will believe in me through their word, that they may all be one. As you, Father, are in me and I am in you, may they also be in us, so that the world may believe that you have sent me. The glory that you have given me I have given them, so that they may be one, as we are one, I in them and you in me, that they may become completely one, so that the world may know that you have sent me and have loved them even as you have loved me. (John 17:20–23)

Here we see that unity is both about reflecting the glory of God and accurately representing God to the unbelieving "world." These two concerns motivate Christians in the Anglican Communion in their desire not only to preserve the unity of their own communion, but to recognize its special vocation to draw together the stray sheep of the world's disparate communions. The church is not simply a means to an end, a boat from which to fish for new disciples or a platform on which to organize for social justice. Ultimately it is called to embody in its own life the redemption that it preaches and the unity-in-diversity it beholds in the triune God. Thus splits in the body are especially damaging for Christians in the Anglican Communion because this body is precisely intended to express and embrace the full diversity of the body of Christ. This is the significance of the words, "He is our peace; in his flesh he has made both groups into one and has broken down the dividing wall, that is, the hostility between us" (Ephesians 2:14). Thus the failure of Christians in the Anglican Communion to remain one body offers a damaging *prima facie* argument that the dividing wall has not been broken down and the gospel is not true.

The word "holy" looks in a different direction. It points to the sanctifying work of the Spirit in making Christians more like God from the inside out. For some Christian traditions, this belief has led to an emphasis on visible holiness; in the contemporary idiom, "If you were accused of being a Christian, would there be enough evidence to convict you?" While there are significant strands of seeking personal sanctification in Anglicanism—particularly in England in the sixteenth and seventeenth centuries, and in the movement that became Methodism in the eighteenth century—the overall tendency has been to perceive holiness in devotional terms, rather than in ethical ones. In other words, holiness has been less about being set apart and more about simply being forgiven. Each regular act of worship (Morning and Evening Prayer, the Holy Eucharist) includes the expectation of a formal confessing of sins and receiving of absolution, which shows how central repentance and forgiveness are to notions of worship among Episcopalians and Anglicans. There is a profound dimension of personal spirituality in the Anglican and Episcopal tradition, but this is less about being set apart and more about attaining a rhythm of life in accord with the rhythm of the saints. Meanwhile, particularly in the wake of the Industrial Revolution, a significant tradition of social holiness evolved, attending to the suffering of the many and the welfare of all; but again, this is less about being the "light of the world," a people distinct and apart, and more about being "the salt of the earth," an incarnational presence in and among.

"Catholic" (which literally means "universal") asks whether the church is as gloriously diverse as God's world. For Episcopalians, "catholic" is not a noun, identifying an individual member of a particular church, but an adjective that points to the wideness of God's mercy. The key to the vision of the Episcopal Church is the claim that the church can be one and catholic at the same time, containing and embracing all God's people and yet at the same time remaining coherent and at peace with itself. Here there are seeds of a significant tension between the vision of the Church of England and that of the rest of the Communion. The Church of England in general understands its vocation as existing for all people residing in England, whether Anglicans, Christians of other denominations, people of other faiths, or those of no expressed faith. Episcopal and Anglican churches in the rest of the world, however, tend to run on a tighter membership system, with a disposition toward mission to, partnership with, and dialogue among those beyond that membership. Churches in the Anglican Communion outside England have found different ways of expressing their catholicity. They, arguably, have to work harder to avoid becoming gatherings of the like-minded, and instead seek to be servants of God's diverse creation. But they share the opportunity and vocation to be churches that seek to reconcile the polarities of Protestant and Catholic, conservative and liberal, personal and political, and to include within themselves a diversity little known elsewhere.

Finally, the term "apostolic" asks the question, would the first apostles recognize us? Those who wish to claim the full catholicity of the Church of England have insisted that, because the bishops became willing partners in Queen Elizabeth I's realignment of the English church during the Reformation, the apostolic succession of the laying-on of hands, going all the way back to Peter, was maintained and the Church of England truly remains not only catholic but apostolic. But this is not the only sense in which the term "apostolic" has been understood. Apostolic also means remaining faithful to the simplicity and sacrifice of the first disciples, and to their teaching and fellowship. In this sense the flourishing of many monastic orders, particularly the Franciscans, who model their lives on the example of the poverty of Christ, keeps the church's apostolicity alive.[10] Episcopal and Anglican scholarship, particularly since the Oxford Movement in the Church of England in the 1830s and beyond, has taken a close interest in the early theologians of the church, such as Irenaeus of Lyons, Athanasius of Alexandria, and Augustine of Hippo; this too preserves an apostolic desire to stay close to the faith of the early church. Finally the term "apostle" means one who is sent out, as a messenger or ambassador, which means that the church, to be apostolic, must constantly set its face to the world in evangelistic and humanitarian mission, sharing and embodying the faith in humble acts of witness and charity. It is, finally, mission that keeps the church apostolic.

Creation and the Kingdom

Creation does not play a large role in the Thirty-Nine Articles: the triune God is simply referred to as the "Maker and Preserver of all things both visible and invisible" (Article I), largely honoring the language of the first article of the Nicene Creed—"Maker of heaven and earth, and of all things visible and invisible." The fact that creation has not been an especially controversial dimension of theology among Episcopalians does not diminish its significance. This may be identified in a number of themes.

Most significantly of all, God was already Trinity—Father, Son, and Holy Spirit—before the creation of the universe. This means three related things.

10. There were 2,154 members of celibate religious orders in the Anglican Communion in 2009. See *Anglican Religious Life 2010–11* (Norwich, England: Canterbury Press, 2009), 24.

First, the Trinity shaped its life to be in relationship with humankind (in Jesus) before there were human beings, before there was a world, indeed a universe, with which to be in relationship. Second, God and the universe are utterly separate from one another; the universe is not made out of God, but is made by God out of nothing. God is not in any sense dependent on the universe, but the universe is completely dependent on God. Third, the character of God is displayed in relationship with the universe. That relationship is entirely one of God's initiative; the making, befriending, and saving of humankind all comes from the overflowing grace of God and is not a necessary, inherent, or automatic dimension of creation. This is the meaning of the term "creation out of nothing": creation had no necessity but was entirely an act of God's grace. God's will to be in relationship becomes the logic of the universe—but that logic is inherent in God, not in the universe. Such logic is consistent with the full revelation of God made in Jesus Christ: that is to say, just as the love of God in the coming of Christ is poured out in suffering and at great cost to God, similarly the love of God in creation is poured out in the focusing of God's unlimited freedom onto the particular realities of the universe. God gives something up in order to wholly love the creation.

Because the creation is the gift of God, it is good. The life that exists within the created order is limited in various ways; its power is finite, its extent is bounded, its flourishing is fragile, its mortality is unavoidable, but nonetheless it is good. Furthermore, the created order is good not just to the extent that human beings can use it for food, shelter, warmth, clothing, or company; it is good for its own sake, whether it relates to human flourishing or not. Nor is it good just to the extent that it is alive, or beautiful, or safe; it is good because God created it. But while good, it is not flawless; perfect flourishing is not an aspect of human experience in creation, and suffering sometimes results from geological or meteorological or countless other characteristics of the created order. Yet while that suffering may render the creation less than perfect, it does not thereby render it less than good. Because of its goodness, there is no place for any fear that the material world is somehow less than the spiritual, that the earth or the body are temporary devices that will be tossed away when fulfillment comes, or that there is some kind of cosmic battle between good and evil whose outcome remains in the balance. St. Paul's proclamation of the resurrection of the body, and the appearance of a new heaven *and a new earth* at the climax of the book of Revelation affirm God's abiding purpose for the material quality of the creation; when evil is one day not simply defeated but utterly cast out, it will not be at the expense of the physical, but its fulfillment.

The creation is an ordered pattern of reflexive relationship, of beings with one another and with God. Thus the term "nature" is inadequate in two senses. On the one hand, to understand any one creature is not simply to discover its "nature" (i.e., its innate qualities) but to see how it coexists with other creatures and its wider environment. Creatures cannot be understood in isolation. On the other hand, "nature" as a whole is not freestanding, nor is it a contained system. It exists in relationship with God—as we have seen, it is the "nature" of God to be so shaped as to be in relationship with the universe. So to say "creation" is not primarily to make a claim or speculation about the origin of the universe, but more significantly to underline that there is no being without God, no sphere of independent existence that operates outside relationship to the Holy Trinity.

This is the heart of Episcopal responses to questions of the beginnings of the universe and the evolution of humankind. The point is not to read the scriptural accounts (notably Genesis 1–2) as a historical and scientific description. It is to see that the triune God is the epitome of relationship, and that God's relationship to the world (and the significance of that relationship) is displayed in Jesus Christ. There may indeed be evolving patterns of "natural selection," but each creature finds its purpose not in survival but in its destiny in relationship to Christ. There may indeed have been a Big Bang that set the universe in motion, but the key question is not where the world is coming from but where it is going, and the answer lies in the fulfillment of relationship with God.

This notion of creation as inherent, ordered relationship is also the heart of Episcopal understandings of ecological concerns. The issue is not that God's purposes might be brought to an untimely end should climate change and species depletion continue unabated, but that creation is fundamentally about mutual interdependence of creatures and their shared environment within the context of relationship with God. Perverting or jeopardizing this coexistence is a profound form of disorder even without the eventual harm to the human species itself.

The themes of creation and kingdom are linked not only because they form the beginning and end of the Christian story, but because they encompass the breadth of God's activity and purpose beyond the revelation of Scripture and the particular witness of Israel and church. The kingdom (or reign) of God refers both to the final unfolding of God's purposes at the end of time and to the anticipatory signs of that unfolding that appeared definitively in Jesus but also continue to appear in the work of the Holy Spirit. These signs are the action of God, but human beings can seek to align themselves with God's action by imitating God's ways in such a manner that they too can perform Spirit-filled anticipatory signs of the kingdom.

Episcopal theologians have tended to distance themselves from both wholly other-worldly and wholly this-worldly notions of the kingdom of God. Because this world is good, and because God will always have a purpose for it, there is no place for dispensationalism, with its idea of successive "dispensations" or periods of history. This account of the coming of the kingdom foresees the precise fulfillment of scriptural texts concerning the number of the elect, their rapture from the earth into the heavens, and the detailed assortment of signs that precede such an apocalyptic future. Because of the abiding character of sin, neither is there a place for a notion of gradual progress that foresees human beings growing nearer to God through moral and social enhancement. The world, while it undoubtedly changes significantly as a result of human endeavor, is not fundamentally better or worse than it was a hundred years ago or will be a hundred years from now. Human endeavor is a vital aspect of faithful discipleship, but fundamental change comes only through God's grace.

Perhaps the most significant principle to maintain in outlining a theology of the kingdom of God is that the face Christians anticipate seeing on the throne on the last day is the face they have already seen on the cross on Good Friday. The first words said at a funeral are often these from the book of Job: "I know that my Redeemer liveth, and that he shall stand at the latter day upon the earth; and though this body be destroyed, yet shall I see God; whom I shall see for myself and mine eyes shall behold, *and not as a stranger.*"11 In other words, Jesus is as much the center of Christian hope as he is the center of Christian memory. The danger of overemphasizing the drama of what God has in store for our future is that it diminishes the definitive character of what has already been revealed in Christ. Meanwhile, if both the definitive significance of Christ in the past and the final revelation of God in the future are downplayed, the inevitable outcome is the exaltation of human endeavor in the present. Episcopal spirituality has most often ensured that the center of attention has remained, not on the moment of personal conversion, nor on the moment of death, nor on the last day, but instead squarely on the days of Christ's birth, crucifixion, and resurrection. Here again is an indication of what an Episcopal emphasis on the incarnation implies.

One characteristic way in which Episcopalians have focused on the future, coming, and entirely God-initiated dimension of the kingdom is by dwelling, through the liturgy and preaching, of Advent, on the "four last things"—death, judgment, heaven, and hell. These are the future ways in which God resolves all that is not right with the world, and completes the story begun in creation.

When the term "kingdom" is used in the present tense, what is not right with the world is broadly divided into two dimensions: that which has a human cause (often described as oppression, or injustice), and that

11. BCP, 469. Emphasis added.

which does not (and yet is still experienced as suffering). The response to both dimensions is rooted in Jesus' ministry. When injustice seems evident, attention dwells upon Jesus' frequent controversies with the Jerusalem authorities, and the way he endorsed and imitated the prophetic ministry of John the Baptist and before him, figures such as Amos and Jeremiah who had called for Israel to be faithful to God by showing mercy to the stranger, the orphan, and the widow. When suffering caused by disease or natural disaster is more prevalent, however, the focus turns to Jesus' healing ministry, particularly the way he reached out to those beyond the bounds of conventional respectability, such as the woman with a hemorrhage or the Samaritan leper.

The parable of the last judgment (Matthew 25:31–46) suggests that, in the end, no firm line may be drawn between these different kinds of disorder. Thus the work of the kingdom is to recognize and meet Jesus in the hungry, thirsty, stranger, naked, sick, or prisoner, not to make distinctions based on how a person came to be so. Such convictions have underwritten widespread charitable work in the Episcopal Church, almost all of which can be read as a response to one or more dimensions of this parable and its clear message. In short, the kingdom of God refers to the way the ministry of Christ and the blessing of the Holy Spirit stretches to the bounds of creation, whether through or in spite of the mission of the church.

Salvation

The axis of the Christian faith is how God enters the disorder of human life in such a way that not only humanity but also the whole creation is redeemed. This redemption has several aspects: the nature of humanity, and the character of its flaws; the way in which Christ's life, death, and resurrection transforms human potential and reality; how this transformation is received; the nature of human flourishing in the power of the Spirit; humankind's ultimate destiny; and the question of whether and to what extent Jesus of Nazareth is the single, central, or indispensable part of this process.

The dignity of humankind resides in that we were the dimension of created existence God chose to assume and embrace in becoming incarnate in Jesus Christ. Thus the key characteristics of human nature are those shared with Jesus; those that are not, notably sin, are not inherent in or integral to human identity. Genesis 1:27 describes how "God created humankind in his image, in the image of God he created them; male and female he created them." This has raised a wide variety of interpretations through the centuries about the sense in which humankind bears God's image. Some have seen it as the capacity to reason; others by the extent of human freedom; others again by the authority delegated in

Genesis 1:28 to "fill the earth and subdue it; and have dominion over the fish of the sea and over the birds of the air and over every living thing that moves upon the earth." But each of these is fulfilled in the coming of Christ, who, as Colossians 1:15–16 declares, is "the image of the invisible God, the firstborn of all creation; for in him all things in heaven and on earth were created, things visible and invisible, whether thrones or dominions or rulers or powers—all things have been created through him and for him." There is no "sanctity of life," as such: there is the sanctity of God, and human life is sacred in that God created it and has chosen to be in relationship with it, most fully and demonstrably in Jesus.

What might it look like for humanity to flourish? One picture that portrays God's destiny for humanity is that offered in Isaiah 65:17–25. Here God speaks of taking "delight in my people" and promises that "no more shall there be in [Jerusalem] an infant that lives but a few days, or an old person who does not live out a lifetime." God foresees that "they shall build houses and inhabit them; they shall plant vineyards and eat their fruit. . . . they shall not labor in vain." Even "the wolf and the lamb shall feed together," because "they shall not hurt or destroy on all my holy mountain." This is a vision of health and well-being, of security, justice, and demanding but fulfilling and fruitful labor, and healthy relationships, between people and each other, people and animals, and people and the soil. This is a comprehensive picture of many dimensions of flourishing life. The one aspect missing here but important to the Old Testament as a whole is worship. A healthy human life is one that worships God rightly, and in doing so finds its place among all things and sets each in their proper station. But crucial to Isaiah's vision is that this flourishing life is what gives God joy: "I am about to create Jerusalem as a *joy*, and its people as a *delight*. I will *rejoice* in Jerusalem, and *delight* in my people" (Isaiah 65:18–19; emphasis added).

One way in which contemporary Episcopal belief has altered from understandings in previous centuries is in the notion of what constitutes a just social order. Once it was quite common to understand women as subject to men, particularly in marriage; to see slavery as acceptable, even appropriate; to view children as potentially wild and needing to be tamed; and to perceive the rich and the poor as assigned to their appropriate sphere in life, perhaps even by God. Today it is usual to reject such understandings and perceive them as signs of humanity gone astray, rather than humanity flourishing. Indeed many Episcopalians sense that it is precisely in the challenging and overcoming of such social structures that Christian mission explicitly lies.

For all the goodness of God's creation, and the richness of God's will for human flourishing, all is not well with humanity and its relationship with God and the creation. The Thirty-Nine Articles are uncompromising in their estimation of the human condition: "Man is very far gone from original righteousness, and is of his own nature inclined to evil, so that the flesh lusteth always contrary to the Spirit; and therefore in every person born into this world, it deserveth God's wrath and damnation" (Article IX). Such a far-reaching judgment of human failure requires some more nuanced delineation of the symptoms and causes of sin.

Sin is living as if there were no God, no grace of God, no creation to remember or kingdom to hope for, no forgiveness to redeem the past or eternal life to focus the future, no faith, no hope, no love. It is living outside the narrative of God—without regard to the creation, the covenant with Israel, the revelation in Christ, the existence of the church, the consummation on the last day—and making one's own narrative instead. Sin comes in two broad forms. On the one hand it arises from ignorance, immaturity, foolishness, lack of insight, clumsiness, hastiness, laziness, and a host of shortcomings that could eventually be ameliorated through thoughtfulness, formation, education, wisdom, and patience. On the other hand sin is utterly perverse and inexplicable: it is turning from glory to sordidness, joy to meanness, beauty to tawdriness, grace to misery. The first kind of sin is a failure of the imagination, an inability to enter and enjoy and inhabit the wondrous world made possible by creation, covenant, and Christ. The second kind of sin is sheer perversity: however propitious the circumstances, however blessed the surroundings, however generous the provision or abundant the resources, humankind will somehow contrive to ruin things. The first kind means people get things wrong however hard they try, while the second recognizes that some of the time, an element within every person has no intention of getting things right.

The simplest summary of the covenant with God offered in the scriptures is Jesus' summary of the Law: "'You shall love the Lord your God with all your heart, and with all your soul, and with all your mind.' This is the greatest and first commandment. And a second is like it: 'You shall love your neighbor as yourself'" (Matthew 22:37–39). Here is the essence of the Christian life: to love God, your neighbor, and yourself. Not wholly to love God is seldom to enter a world without love; more often it is wholly to love something that is not God, and to make a god out of something that did not create and cannot save. This is known as idolatry. Not to love your neighbor is sometimes to fail to trust that God has made adequate provision for both you and your neighbor, and refusing to believe that that there is enough, and that your own flourishing need not involve your neighbor's diminishing. The fear of scarcity is near the root of many forms of sin. But not loving the neighbor can also take a more subtle form. It can be a failure to love yourself, allowing or encouraging your neighbor to take advantage of or oppress you when you should have every reason to stand your ground. The 1662 and the 1979 Books of Common Prayer express this twofold dimension of sin in the General Confession: "We have left undone those things which we ought to have done; and we have done those things which we ought not to have done."

In his treatise *On Christian Doctrine,* Augustine of Hippo made a helpful distinction between those things we "enjoy" and those things we "use." Those things we enjoy never run out, and are an abundant blessing. They are an end in themselves, and to be with them is to be with God. (For Augustine God alone was to be enjoyed; I am developing his ideas here.) Those things we use are largely a means to an end. They do run out, and they are not things we should set our hearts on. Their value is to help us reach, prepare for, value, and understand the things that we are to enjoy. A simple way to describe sin is therefore as follows. To sin is to enjoy things that should properly only be used; and meanwhile merely to use things that should properly be enjoyed. The former is known as idolatry; the latter, ingratitude. In this sense it is easier to see how the noblest act may bear traces of sin, because, short of heaven, scarcely anyone learns how fully to enjoy, and the perverse impulse to use is ineradicable.

How does Jesus save us? The Nicene Creed makes no attempt to answer this often controversial question. It simply says that "for us and for our salvation" Jesus Christ "came down from heaven" and was born, lived, suffered, was buried, rose again, and is seated at the right hand of the Father, whence he will come again to judge and rule forever. There have been broadly five answers to this question that have gained wide influence within the Episcopal Church.[12]

One answer emphasizes Jesus' birth. Jesus saves us by "recapitulating" or reenacting each aspect of our human existence, setting it right as if it were a broken bone. Adam disobeyed God by eating from the tree; Christ obeyed God by dying on the tree. Christ restores every dimension of human life. We are saved because Christ transforms the corruptible, finite quality of human nature by harnessing it to the immortal, incorruptible character of God. Christ also transforms death, in the crucifixion and resurrection, but the incarnation itself is the real moment of salvation.

A second answer emphasizes Jesus' life. It considers humankind as the audience for Jesus' life. In his kindness and generosity, in his ministry to outcasts, sinners, and the sick, in his close relationship to the Father, in his prophetic confrontation with the oppressor, and most of all in his selfless and faithful journey to the cross, Jesus offers himself as the one who transforms our hearts to follow in his steps in the way of sacrificial love. Jesus doesn't seem to change anything about objective reality; it is we who are changed. Thus this theory is sometimes described as "subjective."

12. The following paragraphs closely follow a longer treatment in Wells, *Speaking the Truth,* 155–61.

A third approach focuses on the suffering laid on Jesus as he was tried and hung on the cross. This theory assumes the setting of a court of law. Humanity, the defendant, had accumulated a burden of guilt before God that could never be pardoned, and deserved eternal punishment. But through a unique act of grace, God sent Jesus to face this punishment in our place. This is often called penal substitution. While his death is significant, and the resurrection is not ignored, the theory rests so much on the necessity of punishment that attention often focuses chiefly on the extent of Jesus' sufferings, because it is they, rather than his death, that substitute for the sins of the whole world.

A fourth perspective looks more precisely to Jesus' death itself, a sacrifice that sets right our relationship to God. In this view the problem is essentially one of debt. The most influential view says that the debt is to God's honor; the failure of humanity to do justice before God creates a terrible imbalance in the moral universe. Only humanity *must* pay the debt but only God *can* pay the debt. Hence the God-human, Jesus. When Jesus dies he repays the debt of honor with interest, and it is this interest, known as merit, that humanity can access through the sacraments, and thus find salvation. This is a characteristically Roman Catholic view. An older version of this theory also focused on Jesus' actual death, but saw the debt as owed not to God but to Satan. In this view Adam and Eve had sold humanity to the devil and thus God needed to ransom humanity the way one would redeem a slave. However, Jesus' death, while succeeding as a ransom and buying us back, was in fact a trick because Jesus rose from death and escaped the devil's clutches. Most uses of the word "redemption" hint at this ransom theory.

A fifth answer dwells on Jesus' victorious resurrection. If substitution sees salvation as decided in a law court, then this fifth view sees it as a battle. Death cannot hold Jesus; he destroys death and opens out the prospect of eternal life by rising from the grave. The resurrection of Jesus brings about our resurrection by dismantling the hold of death not just once but for all time. The key word is victory. This is the characteristic Eastern Orthodox view. It has achieved a revival in some parts of the Anglican Communion, particularly among those keen to stress how Jesus' resurrection saves not just the individual soul, but transforms whole societies by dismantling all the social, economic, and cultural forces that oppress people.

One problem with each of these answers is their abstract character, and the way they elide the details of Jesus' life, most notably his Jewishness. One approach that has become influential in Episcopal theology in recent times, and focuses on precisely these details, is to observe how Jesus in his ministry brought people out of exile—death, sickness, social exclusion, fear—and delivered Israel from the exile she had suffered for five hundred years. This is a vision of salvation that emphasizes the corporate over the individual and offers a greater role for the church.

Two terms associated closely with Reformation debates concerning salvation are justification and sanctification. No less than seven of the Thirty-Nine Articles are given over to justification, and they carefully outline how Jesus enables believers to stand before God without fear. There is nothing human beings can do to earn salvation: "We are accounted righteous before God, only for the merit of our Lord and Savior Jesus Christ by Faith, and not for our own works or deservings" (Article XI). The attempt to live a holy life is fruitless in terms of salvation, but is a sign of gratitude and a healthy desire to imitate Christ: "Albeit that Good Works, which are the fruits of Faith, and follow after Justification, cannot put away our sins, and endure the severity of God's judgment; yet are they pleasing and acceptable to God in Christ, and do spring out necessarily of a true and lively Faith insomuch that by them a lively Faith may be as evidently known as a tree discerned by the fruit" (Article XII). But the works of a nonbeliever count for nothing in terms of justification, and "are not pleasant to God": indeed, "for that they are not done as God hath willed and commanded them to be done, we doubt not but they have the nature of sin" (Article XIII). These rather austere writings emphasize the centrality of Christ for salvation. Only Christ is without sin; however worthy human works may be, they do not fit anyone to stand before God. Salvation is therefore an act of pure divine grace and in no sense a human achievement. Yet humans should nonetheless strive to lead a holy life, not as an attempt to secure salvation (which only Christ can do on our behalf), but in reverence for, gratitude toward, and imitation of Jesus.

Our earlier distinction between perversity and lack of imagination may help to clarify the Articles' concerns. When it comes to lack of imagination, the work of the Holy Spirit may gradually heal, transform, amend, refine, and purify human lives so that they may be made holy. This is the process known as sanctification. It receives very little attention in the Thirty-Nine Articles, and is associated less with the Episcopal Church than with Methodism. But human perversity is a failing that can only be addressed by Christ, most specifically in his single sacrificial act on the cross and its transformation through his resurrection. Thus justification, which addresses perversity, is a past achievement of Jesus Christ to which Christians may assent in baptism and in sincere declarations of repentance and faith. Sanctification, on the other hand, is a present and future process, shaped by the activity of the Holy Spirit within the believer and issuing in the fruits of the Spirit, which are "love, joy, peace, patience, kindness, generosity, faithfulness, gentleness, and self-control" (Galatians 5:22–23).

Short of eternal life, what does redeemed existence look like? In addition to the well-being, secure labor, healthy relationships, and joyful worship we saw in our earlier discussion of Isaiah 65, two further aspects of a redeemed life stand out. One is forgiveness. Forgiveness restores the past; eternal life opens out the future. Forgiveness is simply one of a whole series of steps through which God's action in Christ, received through the Holy Spirit, makes it possible for the past to be restored. While the rite of reconciliation, commonly known as "making one's confession," is not universally practiced in the Episcopal Church, it does offer a structure for thinking about forgiveness. The priest reminds the penitent sinner of God's longing to welcome prodigal children home and the rejoicing of the angels at every sinner who repents. The sinner is then invited to tell a truthful story about the past, to express remorse, to commit to setting right what has been put wrong, and to seek to avoid repeating such offenses in the future. The priest then offers counsel, striving to find wisdom in even the most wayward of wanderings, and suggests a penance, a concrete act by which the contrite may express regret and begin to enter new life. Then the priest offers words of forgiveness. The sinner is thus reconciled with God, but is also responsible for reconciling with those they have harmed. This process of trust, truth-telling, penitence, forgiveness, and reconciliation portrays the way forgiveness, rather than being an event, names a process that begins with the proclamation of grace and ends with its fruit.

A second dimension of redeemed existence is the discovery, reception, and exploration of vocation. Vocation is closely tied to baptism: for in baptism, the past is redeemed by the forgiveness of sins and the future is extended in the promise of eternal life. Vocation names the more immediate aspect of that unfolding future. It is a particular calling from God through which believers find their own place in the story of the redemption of all things. It is not necessarily tied, or even closely related, to the duties of a job or the pursuit of a career. Nor is it necessarily static and permanent: it may develop and evolve over time. But it is tailored to a person's unique character and circumstances, and it invariably involves integrating the disparate and often confusing elements of someone's past experiences into a role that only they can perform, a gift that only they can give, a contribution that only they can make. And in a general way that role is called ministry, partly because ministry primarily means service, and, in the words of the collect, God's "service is perfect freedom," but also because all ministry derives from Christ's ministry. Thus Christ's ministry becomes a template for all vocation. Vocations must therefore be expected to take on key characteristics of Christ's ministry—his mission to reconcile all people to God, his willingness to face suffering and sacrifice, and his presence among a close community of believers, among the poor, and in intense dialogue with the powers of his day. A true vocation blends the uniqueness of the believer's character and circumstance with the universal claims of Christ.

But what of *eternal* salvation? What of heaven and hell?[13] Neither the creeds nor the Thirty-Nine Articles offer any details on the life of heaven. The important things to keep in mind about heaven are that it is shaped by the trinitarian God met in Christ; that it is embodied, rather than simply spiritual; and that it is dynamic, rather than static.

To say heaven is shaped by Christ is to dismiss popular and folk conceptions of heaven contained in metaphors such as "I am a thousand winds that blow" or "I have simply passed into the next room." For heaven is not human survival, but the new life received as a pure gift after true and complete death and physical resurrection. The death and resurrection of Christ provides the paradigm for the death and resurrection of the believer: in other words, the resurrected body will bear the scars of wounds received before death, but will also be a body restored, and physically and mentally unburdened of the pain of those scars. Death is real: Christ's resurrection removes its sting, but not its universality. Resurrection is not reabsorption into the infinite: it is distinct, personal existence. Heaven is not the resumption of earthly everyday life, but a state of restored, renewed, and fulfilled relationship with God and one another.

The three most explicit scriptural depictions of heaven are as worship, friendship, and the sharing of food. Images of a banquet abound in the scriptures, and affirm the physical, convivial, and corporate nature of resurrection. Companionship with God, so clearly depicted in the risen Jesus' walk with two grieving disciples on the road to Emmaus in Luke 24, is a restoration of what was lost in the fall. Yet the central image of heaven is that of enjoying and glorifying God forever. Like a choir of diverse voices harmonized in song, each member finds their true fulfillment in a chorus that transcends their individual callings.

There are two broad notions of hell: everlasting agony or total annihilation. The idea of perpetual torment picks up on a good deal of scriptural imagery and maintains the physical dimension of life after death. The second idea of endless isolation and the utter absence of God tends to see hell as the complete evacuation of the good and the real. However, both accounts are problematic when set against the two key attributes of God, who is all-loving and all-powerful. If God is all-loving, how could there be eternal punishment for sin? And if God is all-powerful, how could there be a sphere of existence that perpetually refuses to inhabit the economy of grace? How can there be an eternal estrangement from God that Jesus has not addressed?

The Thirty-Nine Articles are at pains to dispel the "Romish Doctrine concerning Purgatory," which, among other notions, it describes as "a fond thing, vainly invented, and grounded upon no warranty of Scripture, but rather repugnant to the Word of God" (Article XXII). Yet it is

---

13. For a longer treatment of these issues, see Wells, *Speaking the Truth*, 143–55.

hard to reconcile the scriptural imagery of fire and torment and gnashing of teeth with the belief that Jesus displays the character of God, and the conviction that God achieved everything in Jesus, without some notion that Jesus in his suffering on the cross transforms the ugliness of human sin into the beauty of God's grace, and that this is a more demanding and laborious process for some sinners than it is for others.

The Nicene Creed speaks of "the resurrection of the dead, and the life of the world to come" with no specific reference to damnation. Such reticence has become the custom in many parts of the Episcopal Church. Yet removing the crucial moment of God's judgment from the believer's anticipation of death has a significant side effect, which is that the longing for human flourishing and well-being is directed instead toward life on earth. This motivates humanitarian movements to enhance the living conditions of all human beings. But it also changes our sense of death: what was once the gateway to immortality has become the last incongruous insult in a catalogue of apparent injustices that hold human beings back from the ultimate and perpetual earthly fulfillment that they take to be their birthright.

In plural religious cultures, Christians will always be sensitive to the question of whether Jesus is the only way to salvation. This question tends to dominate interreligious dialogue, evoking passionate and polarized convictions. On the one hand it seems out of character for the God of grace and generosity to withhold eternal well-being from not just infants, or those who have never had a chance to hear the gospel, but also those who have been faithful adherents of other faiths or have sought to live what Titus 1:8 calls an "upright and sober life." On the other hand the New Testament assumes that salvation has come uniquely through Jesus, and that is the power and urgency of its evangelistic message. The Thirty-Nine Articles are uncompromising on this point: "Holy Scripture doth set out unto us only the Name of Jesus Christ, whereby men must be saved" (Article XVIII). Moreover so much of St. Paul's teaching emphasizes that God does not judge human beings on the quality of their lives, but looks instead to the comprehensiveness of Jesus' offering and the transparency of the believer's faith. Such ambivalence has meant this question has not received a clear answer in the present generation.

But the key is to keep the emphasis on what heaven is, rather than on who gets there. If heaven is God's gift of everlasting security and well-being and interdependent growth and flourishing, then that is evidently God's will for all creation. But if heaven is more than that—if heaven is intimate companionship with God in Christ, a shape of life made possible by Jesus' cross and resurrection, and expressed in worship and the sharing of food—it is hard to see why anyone who wanted that in the eternal future would not want it in the present too.

CHAPTER 2

The Sources of the Faith

Introduction: Revelation and Authority

How does the Trinity that shapes its life to be in relationship to human beings come to be known, understood, and loved by them? How is a theology such as that developed in the previous chapter arrived at, and on what grounds is anyone to trust it as more than a fanciful rendering of reality? These are questions of revelation and authority, and characteristic Episcopal answers to these questions are the subject of this second part of our study.

Revelation refers to the unveiling of the person, character, and purpose of God. Each term in this definition may be explored further.

"Unveiling" is the more complete disclosure of the God who is already apparent. It is customary to distinguish between two forms of this disclosure. On the one hand there is "natural" (sometimes known as "general") revelation; on the other there is "special" revelation, which indicates all that is not accessible except through the eyes of faith. Episcopal theologians have been more inclined than many others to emphasize natural revelation.

The empirical tradition in English philosophy, which favors observation, experimentation, and experience, coupled with the American pragmatic tradition, which perceives the meaning of a concept in its practical outcomes, steer Anglican and Episcopal theology toward the tangible signs of divine expression. There is good precedent for such convictions in the Bible: Psalm 19:1–2 declares, "The heavens are telling the glory of God; and the firmament proclaims his handiwork. Day to day pours forth speech, and night to night declares knowledge." The Old Testament figure of Job is constantly scouring the creation for signs of God's benevolent hand. Job declares:

He is wise in heart, and mighty in strength
—who has resisted him, and succeeded?—
he who removes mountains, and they do not know it,
when he overturns them in his anger;
who shakes the earth out of its place,
and its pillars tremble;
who commands the sun, and it does not rise;
who seals up the stars;
who alone stretched out the heavens
and trampled the waves of the Sea;
who made the Bear and Orion,
the Pleiades and the chambers of the south;
who does great things beyond understanding,
and marvelous things without number. (Job 9:4–10)

And in the New Testament Paul bases his argument among the Athenians on identifying the God whom they already know, but have not yet named:

For as I went through the city and looked carefully at the objects of your worship, I found among them an altar with the inscription, "To an unknown god." What therefore you worship as unknown, this I proclaim to you. The God who made the world and everything in it, he who is Lord of heaven and earth, does not live in shrines made by human hands. (Acts 17:23–24)

This is an example of natural theology.

On the other hand, revealed theology, or special revelation as it is sometimes called, directs attention to the specific characteristics of God that are not accessible to the ordinary human senses. These include identifying God as Trinity, the naming of the three persons of the Trinity as Father, Son, and Holy Spirit, the incarnation of Jesus Christ, the life of the church in the power of the Holy Spirit, the form and process of salvation, and the hope of everlasting life with God.

The threefold formulation "Scripture, tradition, and reason" is the characteristic model in the Episcopal Church for perceiving revelation and understanding authority. The crucial point to grasp about this understanding of revelation is that in the customary formulation of Scripture, tradition, and reason, *all three* are regarded as forms of revelation.

It is not that Scripture comprises revelation, tradition describes imple-mentation, and reason amasses all the questions or new information that are in tension with Scripture and tradition. It is that Scripture, tradition, and reason are complementary and overlapping sources of revelation. They are not inherently in tension with one another; rather, these are three dimensions of the way the church discovers and rediscovers who God is, what God's purpose for creation is, and what is made possible by God's redemption in Christ.

Today the term "experience" is often added as a fourth dimension, but this is based on a misunderstanding of Scripture, tradition, and reason. None of these three forms of revelation is self-explanatory: each comes to be understood as it is interpreted in the life of a community of faith. In other words, experience is simply another name for the interpretative process by which the church comes to receive revelation from Scripture, tradition, and reason. Therefore to set experience up as a fourth source of authority is im-mediately to assume a tension between it and one or more of the previous three. Instead, experience should be regarded as an aspect of Scripture, in that the Bible was recorded, collected, and edited by communities of faith as they experienced the work of the Holy Spirit. By the same token, tradition means the distilled history and wisdom of communities seeking to embody Scripture, while reason refers to the ways communities have sought to trans-late their knowledge of the world into the language of Scripture, and their knowledge of Scripture into the language of the world. In other words, all three emerged, and are still emerging, in gradual dialogue with experience.

This emphasis on communal discernment is vital to the understanding of revelation and authority. Prayer is common, or corporate, and discern-ment of Scripture—the principal authority—takes place in the context of this common prayer. Thus the English Reformation theologian Rich-ard Hooker, the most-cited source on these matters in the Anglican tradition, describes the process for coming to a common mind on mat-ters about which Scripture is silent or unclear. He says that if there is a consensus of persons of moderate judgment, who believe that proposed readings are neither unjust nor unreasonable; and that those interpreta-tions of Scripture promote godliness, have been sanctioned by ecclesias-tical tradition, or have been approved by the legitimate authority of the church; then it is appropriate for the community to affirm them. A key test of this approach came when the Episcopal Church was founded after the Revolutionary War and decisions needed to be made about how it should understand authority. It committed itself to having bishops, and to a set form of common prayer, while remaining open to local variation in matters "inessential" that did not contradict Scripture.[1]

---

1. I am grateful to Craig Uffman for helping me clarify the thoughts in this paragraph.

One scriptural story that illuminates the relationship between natural and revealed theology is Matthew's account of the birth of Jesus (2:1–12). The wise men beheld a star in the heavens: here is the language of natural revelation. They responded and made their way to Jerusalem. Thus it is possible to be drawn toward God without Scripture. The wise men were close to the truth of Christ's birth, but a miss was as good as a mile. Without Scripture, it is not possible to know the heart of God, to meet the incarnate Jesus. When the wise men came to Jerusalem, however, the scribes explored the Hebrew scriptures and found that the Messiah was to be born in Bethlehem—here is a moment of special revelation. The wise men then made their way to Bethlehem to find something natural revelation could never have disclosed: a vulnerable baby, born in humble circumstances, yet proclaimed as the Son of God. The story thus portrays the two kinds of revelation harmoniously balanced in bringing people face-to-face with God. It offers a model for Christian understandings of other forms of knowledge, such as science, and of other forms of faith, such as Islam and Buddhism. The lesson of the wise men story is that general revelation may get one to "Jerusalem"; only special revelation may get one that short but crucial extra step to "Bethlehem."

How does revelation take place? This is one of the most pressing questions for Christians seeking to discover and respond obediently to God's character and will. One may speak of four modes, or moments, of revelation, each of which is extensively exhibited in Scripture.

First of all, there are momentary and dramatic divine interventions. There are many such moments in Scripture, several of which are associated with the call of a prophet or servant of God. In the Old Testament perhaps the most vivid moment occurs when moving fingers appear at the feast of the Chaldean King Belshazzar and write words on the wall, which Daniel interprets to mean the king's overthrow that very night (Daniel 5:1–30). Another example is that of the prophet Elijah, who, when hiding on Mt. Horeb, does not find God in the earthquake, the wind, or the fire, but in the ensuing sound of an echoing silence (1 Kings 19:11–18). One striking event in the New Testament is the appearance of the angel Gabriel to Mary, announcing that she will bear a son, but perhaps the definitive among such moments is the account of the conversion of Paul on the road to Damascus:

> Suddenly a light from heaven flashed around him. He fell to the ground and heard a voice saying to him, "Saul, Saul. . . . I am Jesus, whom you are persecuting." . . . Saul got up from the ground, and though his eyes were open, he could see nothing; so they led him by the hand and brought him into Damascus. For three days he was without sight, and neither ate nor drank. . . . Ananias . . . laid his hands on Saul and said, "Brother Saul, the Lord Jesus, who appeared to you on your way here, has sent

me so that you may regain your sight and be filled with the Holy Spirit."
And immediately something like scales fell from his eyes, and his sight
was restored. Then he got up and was baptized. (Acts 9:3–18)

Stories of similar intensity have continued to be told throughout the history of the church, but they have never been considered normative for all
other forms of revelation. Three other kinds of divine disclosure stand
alongside this highly dramatic form.

One is the carefully established and regular practices of embodied
devotion, such as personal and corporate prayer and worship, Bible
study, pilgrimage, fasting, and being present among the poor, the prisoner, the sick, and the dying. These are places where the faithful may
expect to come face-to-face with God, whether they are aware of it or
not. An example of a conscious encounter with God during a regular act
of piety is Zechariah's experience when he is chosen by lot to enter the
Temple sanctuary and offer incense. An angel appears and announces
that Zechariah and his wife Elizabeth will have a son named John (Luke
1:5–23). An example of unintentional divine encounter is described by
Jesus in his parable of the last judgment:

> Then the righteous will answer him, "Lord, when was it that we saw
> you hungry and gave you food, or thirsty and gave you something to
> drink? And when was it that we saw you a stranger and welcomed you,
> or naked and gave you clothing? And when was it that we saw you sick
> or in prison and visited you?" And the king will answer them, "Truly I
> tell you, just as you did it to one of the least of these who are members
> of my family, you did it to me." (Matthew 25:37–40)

The gathering of the councils of the church is one of the "regular" places
where revelation may be expected, and for this reason the early ecumenical councils, where the creeds were worked out and articulated, are assigned a special authority.

The third way in which revelation is disclosed is through retrospection. Sometimes a pattern can appear when a series of historical events are
viewed as a whole; when set alongside one another, one can sometimes see
a pattern that was not so apparent when these events were taking place. In
the Old Testament, for example, Psalm 78 describes an ordered sequence
of acts of God that create a cumulative message of God's purpose and
faithfulness. In the New Testament we can see a similar litany of blessing
outlined in the series of those who acted "by faith" in Hebrews 11—Abel,
Enoch, Noah, Abraham, Sarah, Rahab, and many more.

The fourth and ultimate form of revelation is the full disclosure of
God on the last day, a prospect anticipated at many places in the New
Testament and most amply in the book of Revelation. This apocalyptic

vision is rendered vividly in the words of Charles Wesley's Advent hymn, "Lo, He Comes with Clouds Descending":

> Every eye shall now behold Him
> Robed in dreadful majesty;
> Those who set at naught and sold Him,
> Pierced and nailed Him to the tree,
> Deeply wailing, deeply wailing,
> Shall the true Messiah see.[2]

Anglicanism was born amid a crisis of authority as the Reformation pitted the custom of ancient tradition and vested office against the appeal to *sola scriptura,* "Scripture alone." Placing Scripture first in the threefold formula is a significant gesture to the Protestant side of this Reformation debate. By following Scripture with tradition, however, Episcopalians make a similar nod in a Catholic direction. Just as the Reformation made it problematic to assert the authority of tradition over Scripture, so the Enlightenment severely criticized inherited authority—and thus both the Bible and tradition—preferring to prize reason above all things. By including reason in its threefold formula, the Episcopal Church acknowledges the challenge of the Enlightenment but indicates that reason never exists in the abstract. Every question and every critical inquiry arises out of some kind of tradition.

Scripture

The Thirty-Nine Articles make a confident statement about which books constitute Holy Scripture. "In the name of the Holy Scripture we do understand those canonical Books of the Old and New Testament, of whose authority was never any doubt in the Church" (Article VI). By "never any doubt" the Articles refer to the process of reception by which the early church came to recognize the books of the Old Testament and the New, a process largely complete in the late second century. (There was plenty of doubt before that.) The exact list was not finalized (to include Jude, 2 Peter, and 1, 2, and 3 John) until the fourth century. The authoritative books are known as the canon, which comes originally from an Egyptian word meaning *reed,* and coming more broadly to mean "rule" or "norm." The make-up of the New Testament ceased to be a source of controversy in the fourth century. While there exist a number of writings from the first two centuries that describe the life of Christ or list sayings or reflections, such as the *Epistle of Barnabas* or the *Shepherd of Hermas,* these have not been regarded as authoritative.

2. *The Hymnal 1982,* 57.

One controversial and unresolved area, however, concerns precisely which books constitute the Old Testament. The thirty-nine Jewish books that are written in Hebrew form the undisputed Old Testament; meanwhile, Greek versions of the Old Testament (the Septuagint) include between eleven and fourteen additional Jewish books written in Greek, which were excluded by most Jews from 90 CE onward. These books, which came to be known collectively as the Apocrypha ("hidden away"), were generally recognized by the whole church prior to the Reformation, but have not been considered canonical by most Protestant traditions since. In a characteristic compromise, the Thirty-Nine Articles name two additional books, 1 and 2 Esdras, among the books of the Old Testament, and then list the rest of the pre–New Testament books separately, accompanied by the phrase, "the other Books. . . the Church doth read for example of life and instruction of manners; but yet doth it not apply them to establish any doctrine" (Article VI). These books are usually printed separately from the Old Testament books, and some congregations read them occasionally in worship in place of the Old Testament lesson.

One error the Thirty-Nine Articles are quick to dispel is any suggestion that the Old Testament lacks authority, or has been superseded by the New Testament in the coming of Christ. The articles insist, "The Old Testament is not contrary to the New: for both in the Old and New Testament everlasting life is offered to Mankind by Christ" (Article VII). Episcopal theology makes no concession to the false notion that the Old Testament God is a God of war, or rule, or tribe, in contrast with the New Testament God of peace, grace, and all humanity. Rather, the Old Testament *is* the gospel, and God speaks in it and through it and from it. However, a more subtle approach is employed in relation to the very large numbers of rules and commandments offered in the Torah (the first five books of the Old Testament). Following the twelfth-century Jewish scholar Maimonides, and in keeping with much Reformation thought, the Articles of Religion make the following distinction: "Although the Law given from God by Moses, as touching Ceremonies and Rites, do not bind Christian men, nor the Civil precepts thereof ought of necessity to be received in any commonwealth; yet notwithstanding, no Christian man whatsoever is free from the obedience of the Commandments which are called Moral" (Article VII). This distinction between the moral, ceremonial, and civil commandments is widely upheld today, although disputes arise as to which category certain commandments (such as some of those pertaining to sexual expression) truly belong, and the distinction itself relies on an anachronistic division of categories unknown to the Old Testament imagination.

What is it that turns these particular written words into Holy Scripture? The notion of the authority of Scripture is a way of talking about two claims—and sometimes about a third, less helpful assertion. What is really at stake is the authority of God, which means that God is the source of all that is good, right, true, and beautiful, the creator and sustainer of all things, and the origin and destiny of everything dead, living, and yet to be. The second and subsidiary claim is that the Bible is the unique and comprehensive witness to the God who has such authority. This is largely a statement about the inspiration of Scripture. But it also implies that the Bible gives us a way of interpreting all other forms of knowledge and discerning all other kinds of wisdom. One can, for example, see the Bible as telling a story in five parts: creation, covenant, Christ, church, and consummation (the end of all things).[3] This story distills the witness of the Old and New Testaments and locates us, the church, in the fourth part of a five-part narrative, thus giving us a sense of where we fit in God's purposes. The less helpful assertion, however, is that Scripture has an authority that transcends (or excludes) all other authority, including tradition or reason. Such an assumption neglects to recognize that every reading of Scripture is an act of interpretation that requires attention to earlier readings (tradition) and of the wider discernment of the church (reason). It is an assumption that tends to arise out of a legitimate fear that tradition or reason has strayed too far from Scripture itself, but at the same time it does not always focus on the authority of God the Trinity made known in Christ through the Holy Spirit in the world and in the church.

If the question of authority rests partly, perhaps largely, on a notion of inspiration, what then does it mean to regard the thirty-nine books of the Old Testament and twenty-seven books of the New as inspired? To speak of inspiration is to refer to the action of the Holy Spirit in regard to the Bible. There are three broad ways to conceive of scriptural inspiration. Since the Thirty-Nine Articles were first issued in 1563, the Bible has begun to be studied and interpreted with a host of new methods and tools. Episcopalians have in general been less discomfited by these new methods and tools than most other Christians. The various critical methods, and the responses to them, can be arranged according to their respective understandings of scriptural inspiration.

One understanding is to look behind the text to see inspiration in *the events the text describes.* Thus Moses and the children of Israel crossing the Red Sea is the important thing: the account of the event in Exodus 14–15 may or may not include some eccentricities and incongruities, but what matters is the event itself. This view sees the text as the best available witness to a series of uniquely inspired events and divine communications. This view has difficulty adjusting to more complex parts of the

---

3. For an extensive treatment of this notion of authority, see Samuel Wells, *Improvisation: The Drama of Christian Ethics* (Grand Rapids: Brazos, 2004), especially 53–57.

Bible that make no claim to historical fact (such as the book of Job), because it is so tied to seeing Christianity as constituted by a sequence of historical events.

The major strength of this approach is that it has proved adaptable to a number of different kinds of critical methods. Source criticism attempts to identify the places or documents from which the scriptural authors derived their material, such as a theoretical collection of Jesus' sayings that was available to Matthew and Luke but not to Mark, while form criticism breaks the scriptures down into units of differing genres (such as poem, hymn, or parable) and speculates on the nature and pattern of those genres. Redaction criticism seeks to characterize the authors of the texts themselves, including their particular theological interests, the communities from which they arose, and the needs they sought to meet by writing the texts. Meanwhile, historians and archaeologists also seek to find evidence to corroborate or challenge the historical validity of texts that refer to specific events and persons.

These methods all seek to find the world *behind* the scriptural text. The empirical tradition in British thinking and the pragmatic tradition in American culture and philosophy both incline Episcopalians and Anglicans to be prepared to detach the scriptural accounts somewhat from the events they describe. This creates three dimensions instead of what had been one. That is to say, whereas there had once been only the event-as-recorded-in-Scripture, there is now (1) the event as witnessed by other authorities—such as extrabiblical sources—and partially reconstructed; (2) the scriptural account itself, whose value goes far beyond bare historical veracity, which is itself a relatively recent notion, largely unknown to the scriptural authors; and (3) the intersection between the two. Many find this complexity bewildering, and either long for or insist on a return to the earlier conviction that Scripture is always a precise record of historical events. Nonetheless, Episcopal scholars have generally been adaptable and able to feel at home in all three of these dimensions.

A second understanding of inspiration is to look to the text itself to see inspiration in *the very words themselves*. Thus the psalms were inspired in their composition, and any reader who comes to them with a pure heart, ready to receive their wisdom, may expect to glean from them abiding truth. Likewise if Jesus in one place says "Whoever is not against us is for us" (Mark 9:40), and in another place, "Whoever is not with me is against me" (Luke 11:23), the point is not to discover which of the sayings is the more likely to be historically attestable, but to consider both as authentic and authoritative. A more extreme version of this approach is to see the Scripture as infallible—in other words, to regard every word of the Scripture as equally sound, and not to entertain any possibility that it might misrepresent history or misdirect future conduct. Another related assumption is that the Bible possesses a single, plain meaning that is accessible to any reader in any context.

In scholarly terms the approach of looking at the text itself is associated with literary criticism, which considers the final form of the text without regard to authorial intent or textual emendations. Forms of literary criticism applied to the Bible include narrative criticism, which addresses plot, character, and other such elements; rhetorical criticism, which studies the way a text shapes its audience; and canonical criticism, which considers the text in the light of the whole canon of scripture of which it is a part.

A third perspective is to locate inspiration in *the life of a community that seeks to embody the text*. In this view the two things that matter most are the God of Jesus Christ and the faithfulness of those who seek to live the gospel. In other words, the precise details of the saving events and the sacred word (in short, the Bible) are not worth fighting over, because neither decisively shape what is more important—the character of God and of the believer. Securing the authority of the exact words of Scripture is no guarantee of securing these vital elements of the faith. It is unusual to hold this perspective alone, it being more often combined with one or both of the previous approaches.

Those who adhere to the second view, that inspiration lies in the text itself, may be inclined to criticize those who hold the first and third on the grounds that they are treating the Bible as no more than a means to an end, without giving the scriptures the veneration they deserve. Advocates of the first and third approaches may counter that this is precisely how the Bible should be regarded—as a means, albeit perhaps the most significant means—to the end of meeting the God of Jesus Christ in historical revelation and in the church today. To place higher value on the scriptures than that, they might argue, is to risk making them the focus of idolatry, for it is God, not the scriptures, that should be truly venerated. The most quoted Bible verses in the debate are these: "All scripture is inspired by God and is useful for teaching, for reproof, for correction, and for training in righteousness, so that everyone who belongs to God may be proficient, equipped for every good work" (2 Timothy 3:16–17). These verses can be adopted readily by proponents of each of the three views.

The characteristic approach of the Episcopal Church has been to see wisdom in all three perspectives. While for much of their history the sacredness of the text itself has been taken for granted, the fact that Episcopalians have remained open to the first interpretation and, more recently, to the third, has meant that they have struggled less than many Protestant denominations over the last 150 years with the impact of historical and textual criticism of the Bible. A tradition that put all its emphasis on the inspiration of the words themselves would be much more vulnerable at points where their historical veracity or theological consistency came to be questioned. By contrast Episcopal tradition has generally held a broader notion of authority in relation to Scripture, and this has made it more adept in the face of such criticism.

One of the most famous lines in the Thirty-Nine Articles, echoed later in the Chicago-Lambeth Quadrilateral, runs as follows: "Holy Scripture containeth all things necessary to salvation" (Article VI). This notion is known as the "sufficiency" of Scripture. At first glance it might seem as though this statement contravenes the balance of Scripture, tradition, and reason by placing all the emphasis on Scripture. But this is not the way it is usually interpreted. The point is that God has been fully revealed in Christ, and that Christ re-presents all that God made plain to Israel, and discloses God's restoration of the created order. There is nothing missing here. Any *addition* to what God has done in Christ would in fact be a *subtraction*, because it would diminish the faith that God in Christ has done everything needful and more. Thus tradition and reason may amplify and clarify, order and embody what is disclosed in Scripture, but not add to, alter, or contradict what is found there.

Episcopalians have tended to take this notion of "sufficiency" in broad and general terms, rather than precise and specific ones. Thus Scripture is taken as the witness to the shape of history—creation, covenant, Christ, church, consummation; and the particular details of Christ's coming, death, and resurrection—but the specifics, other than those concerning Christ, have been scrutinized less carefully. So, for example, it is customary in the Episcopal Church to regard the opening chapters of Genesis as a narrative that outlines God's originating purpose, along with human foolishness and fragility, but not to seek there a detailed historical account of universal or planetary origins. Likewise the book of Revelation and the second half of the book of Daniel are generally seen as a vivid challenge to the church's relationship with earthly powers and a call to wait in hope for the coming of God's just, final, and transforming reign. But they are not regarded as an account of the precise stages involved in the identification and preservation of an elect 144,000 souls as the rest of humanity goes to its doom. When the Bible is used in Christian ethics, whether the subject is genetics, ecology, or politics, we seldom expect an exact prescription for a pressing dilemma or crisis. Nonetheless, the sufficiency of Scripture is witnessed in the expectation that—whether the theme is the goodness of creation, humanity made in the image of God, the Spirit's call to conversion, Christ's incarnational faithfulness with all people, the cost of discipleship, or the power of the resurrection—Scripture as discerned by the tradition and reason of the church through the Holy Spirit will once again give God's people everything they need.

Tradition

The New Testament did not write itself, nor did it float down, complete and polished, from the sky. It was written by the early church, as its members were called to record the memories and practices of the apostles and the communities they founded in the power of the Spirit. Not only was Scripture tradition before it was Scripture, but elements of the earlier tradition are still visible in the Bible itself. For example, Paul's description of the humility of Christ (Philippians 2:6–11), which begins, "who, though he was in the form of God, did not regard equality with God as something to be exploited, but emptied himself, taking the form of a slave, being born in human likeness," is widely regarded as deriving from an earlier hymn. Many believe it was not written by Paul himself, but lodged in the tradition that emerged in the twenty-five years between the ascension of Christ and Paul's writing of the letter to the Philippians. Thus it was tradition in the form of historical events, memories of Jesus, theological reflection, and the reinterpretation of the Old Testament that gave us Scripture.

But what is the status of tradition (or, better, traditions, for tradition is not and never could be a homogeneous unit) once the core of the tradition has been crystallized in the New Testament? This is one of the most controversial questions the church has faced, and a question that was at the heart of the Reformation. To answer it we need to offer a more complex account of what is meant by tradition.

The traditions of the church are those teachings and practices, beyond but not necessarily in contradiction to the words of Scripture, which have accumulated over the centuries and have stood the test of time. We may observe a number of kinds of these traditions.

One is the teachings and practices that go back to earliest times, and seem to be more or less contemporary with the New Testament texts. Several prominent early Christian writers such as Irenaeus, Tertullian, and Origen refer to a "Rule of Faith" that was apparently in wide circulation but does not seem to have survived antiquity. The anthem widely sung in eucharistic worship, which begins "Glory to God on high, and on earth peace, good will toward men. We praise thee, we bless thee, we worship thee, we glorify thee, we give thanks to thee for thy great glory, O Lord God, heavenly King, God the Father Almighty. . . ." is one of several hymns from a similar period, along with the anthem known as the *Te Deum*, which begins, "We praise thee, O God; we acknowledge thee to be the Lord," and is often sung at Morning Prayer. Another very early text is the Apostles' Creed, which arose within the context of the liturgy of baptism, but for which there is no known place or time or origin. Meanwhile, the words "For thine is the kingdom, the power, and the glory, forever and ever. Amen" begin to appear appended to the Lord's Prayer in some later manuscripts of Matthew.

While the central sacraments of baptism and eucharist are explicitly cited in the New Testament, the elaborations of their celebration seem to be a similar and very early development of the church. Thus they take their place alongside ancient developments not precisely recorded in Scripture but that are more or less complementary to the scriptural witness.

A second aspect of tradition refers to those teachings and practices that emerged more formally, especially those that did so during the undivided period in the church's history prior to the split between East and West in 1054, and in particular the seven ecumenical councils at which the whole church was represented: Nicaea (325), Constantinople (381), Ephesus (431), Chalcedon (451), the Second Council of Constantinople (553), the Third Council of Constantinople (680), and the Second Council of Nicaea (787).[4] The creed of Nicaea (in the form that emerged from the first council of Constantinople) and the definition of Chalcedon are the most explicit examples of this formal tradition. Whether the threefold order of ministry—bishop, priest, and deacon—can be found in Scripture, or has emerged through tradition, is a matter on which people differ.

One document that offers a characteristic and influential understanding of tradition in the Episcopal Church is the Chicago-Lambeth Quadrilateral of 1886. It is a statement on ecumenism issued by bishops of the Episcopal Church gathered in Chicago and subsequently distilled into Resolution 11 of the Lambeth Conference of all Anglican bishops in 1888. The Quadrilateral is an example of tradition as dynamic and ongoing discernment, wisdom, experience, and practice, as well as the process of reception, by which the validity of tradition is established in the church. In its latter form, it regards the following four criteria as the basis for the reunion of the churches:

(a) The Holy Scriptures of the Old and New Testaments, as "containing all things necessary to salvation," and as being the rule and ultimate standard of faith.

(b) The Apostles' Creed, as the Baptismal Symbol; and the Nicene Creed, as the sufficient statement of the Christian faith.

(c) The two Sacraments ordained by Christ Himself—Baptism and the Supper of the Lord—ministered with unfailing use of Christ's words of Institution, and of the elements ordained by Him.

(d) The Historic Episcopate, locally adapted in the methods of its administration to the varying needs of the nations and peoples called of God into the Unity of His Church.[5]

4. The Roman Catholic Church recognizes a further fourteen ecumenical councils, including the Fourth Lateran Council (1215), the Council of Trent (1545–63), and the Second Vatican Council (1965), but those have not been given the same authority in Episcopal circles.

5. BCP, 877–78.

These four points summarize what Episcopalians mean by tradition and how it sits alongside the authority of Scripture. But this is not all that tradition means, for there are two further dimensions of the use of the term that need to be identified.

One is an almost technical term associated with the so-called Catholic Revival, whose most eloquent expression is found in the Oxford Movement within the Church of England, beginning in the 1830s but with an influence that reaches up to the present day. When the Tractarians (as early members of this movement were known) employed the term "tradition," they were referring explicitly to the revered works of the theologians of the first five centuries, whom they called, collectively, the "Fathers." These church fathers may be grouped into three categories, beginning with the apostolic fathers, who wrote around or shortly after the time of the composition of the New Testament, among them Clement of Rome, Ignatius of Antioch, and Polycarp. Then there are the eastern fathers who wrote in Greek—Irenaeus, Clement of Alexandria, Origen, Athanasius, Basil of Caesarea, Gregory of Nazianzus, and Gregory of Nyssa. Finally there are the western fathers who wrote in Latin, notably Tertullian, Ambrose, Augustine of Hippo, and Gregory the Great. Whereas Lutherans might look to Martin Luther as the touchstone of their theology and faith, and the Reformed might look to John Calvin, the Tractarians' devotion to the early theologians of the church inspired a great many Anglicans and Episcopalians to do the same, seeing them as the exemplars of everything that extended, explored, examined, and embodied the witness of the scriptures and might thus fit the description "tradition." The Tractarians would have recognized their own convictions in the succinct phrase of the contemporary theologian Jaroslav Pelikan, who describes tradition as not the dead faith of the living, but the living faith of the dead.[6]

During the Reformation, Protestants accused Catholics of "adding to" the faith, while Catholics accused Protestants of setting aside historic practice and custom. The central Tractarian figure John Henry Newman, in a highly influential essay in 1845, pointed out that doctrine had never been and could never be unchangeable, but that did not mean it must become corrupt; instead he outlined what he called the "development" of Christian doctrine, and the concern to keep the church as much like that of the fathers as possible. This conviction led him to become a Roman

---

6. "Tradition is the living faith of the dead, traditionalism is the dead faith of the living. And, I suppose I should add, it is traditionalism that gives tradition such a bad name. The reformers of every age, whether political or religious or literary, have protested against the tyranny of the dead, and in doing so have called for innovation and insight in place of tradition." Jaroslav Pelikan, *The Vindication of Tradition: 1983 Jefferson Lecture in the Humanities* (New Haven: Yale University Press, 1984), 65.

Catholic, not least because such a view of development requires a living authority, which he came to see as the principal rationale for the papacy. Henceforth all accounts of tradition in the Episcopal Church have been mindful of Newman's journey.

Finally, but perhaps most significantly, one more dimension is very evident in the Thirty-Nine Articles, which, despite their emphasis on Scripture, are deeply conscious of tradition as a complementary strand of authority. They are alert to the danger of tradition:

> It is not lawful for the Church to ordain any thing that is contrary to God's Word written, neither may it so expound one place of Scripture, that it be repugnant to another. Wherefore, although the Church be a witness and a keeper of Holy Writ, yet, as it ought not to decree any thing against the same, so besides the same ought it not to enforce any thing to be believed for necessity of Salvation. (Article XX)[7]

This is a clear warning against the excesses of the Catholic Church as the reformers saw them. But later in the Articles comes a much more positive understanding of tradition:

> It is not necessary that Traditions and Ceremonies be in all places one, or utterly like; for at all times they have been divers, and may be changed according to the diversity of countries, times, and men's manners, so that nothing be ordained against God's Word. Whosoever, through his private judgment, willingly and purposely, doth openly break the Traditions and Ceremonies of the Church, which be not repugnant to the Word of God, and be ordained and approved by common authority, ought to be rebuked openly, (that others may fear to do the like,) as he that offendeth against the common order of the Church, and hurteth the authority of the Magistrate, and woundeth the consciences of the weak brethren. Every particular or national Church hath authority to ordain, change, and abolish, Ceremonies or Rites of the Church ordained only by man's authority, so that all things be done to edifying. (Article XXXIV)[8]

Gone is the fierce suspicion of tradition as liable to displace Scripture. In its place we find an understanding of traditions and ceremonies in the plural, accentuating the healthy diversity of the church, which is worthy of the loyalty and adherence of the faithful. And here also is a nuanced appreciation for local discernment, based around the principle set forth in 1 Corinthians 14: that all things be done for the building up of the church and the faithful—in short, for "edifying."

Whereas the previous two understandings of tradition emphasize the church's divine orientation, this one is rooted more in the human reality

7. BCP, 871.
8. BCP, 874.

of the church. Many of the features of church culture within the Episcopal Church belong to local custom, practical wisdom, and particular circumstance, including the clothing, titles, and vestments of its clergy, the architecture and furnishings of its buildings, the liturgical shape and rituals of its church year, the shape and substance of its prayer books, the nature of its theological and ministerial training, and the character and order of its councils, synods, and general governance. The irony is that such matters are perhaps more frequently the focus of passionate disagreement among Christians than matters of Scripture and doctrine. (The biggest argument I have ever been called to arbitrate in a congregation was about a stained-glass window.)

A more positive perspective on this aspect of tradition that incorporates and blesses local wisdom and custom appears in regard to prayer. There is no doubt that Scripture offers a host of prayers, including "The Lord bless you and keep you; the Lord make his face to shine upon you, and be gracious to you; the Lord lift up his countenance upon you, and give you peace" (Numbers 6:24–26), and the Lord's Prayer. Yet it also goes without saying, both that such prayers do not exhaust the range of spirituality, and that other words and styles of prayer have, through long cherishing, become close to the heart of faith. For example the Collect for Purity, which begins, "Almighty God, to whom all hearts are open, all desires known, and from whom no secrets are hid" has an honored place in Episcopal devotion, and indeed the whole body of collects that populate the Book of Common Prayer are widely regarded as among Anglican liturgy's greatest gifts to the universal church. It is easy to forget that the rhythm of Morning and Evening Prayer, as set out in the prayer book, is a tradition rooted in the unique practice of the Church of England and thus distinct to the Anglican Communion—one that is soaked in Scripture, but nonetheless has a shape and order that has arisen through custom and circumstance.

Reason

I have referred more than once to the pragmatic, empirical strand in British and American ways of seeing the world. This has several theological grounds. Most especially it lies in the spirit of a conviction about Christ's incarnation. Jesus embraced all the contingencies and circumstances of human existence; thus paying attention to the particulars of embodied human life in the world naturally follows as part of the response of faith. More broadly this strand draws on a view of creation as the theater of God's glory, as well as the healthy aspiration to discern the trace of God's hand in the pattern of the workings and relationships within the universe. But it also looks to the Holy Spirit, through whom the God of Jesus Christ becomes known in all manner of places and aspects of life.

Thus to speak of "reason" as the third aspect of authority—and the third dimension of revelation—is to draw attention to a number of ways in which God is made known, and in which humankind appropriately responds to God, which complement what is expressed through Scripture and tradition. It is also to expect that these two may be rendered in an orderly and "reasonable" fashion, which does not simply fall back on mystery and paradox in the face of the complex and challenging aspects of faith. To uphold reason also shows a healthy respect for human faculties and investigations, so that revelation may be seen as working with the grain of human wisdom, and not always in contradiction to it.

Closer attention to the sixth of the Thirty-Nine Articles reveals that this tenor in Anglican and Episcopal theology has been present from the beginning. After maintaining that Holy Scripture contains everything necessary for salvation, this clarification follows: "So that whatsoever is not read therein, nor may be proved thereby, is not to be required of any man, that it should be believed as an article of the Faith, or be thought requisite or necessary to salvation" (Article VI). Theologian Stephen Sykes offers a helpful amplification of what this means for the balance of Scripture, tradition, and reason: "[The Article] is not saying that everything which can be read in scripture ought to be believed; but rather that what a plain reader cannot himself find in the text can in no circumstances be required of him as an article of belief."[9] Here we begin to see what a healthy relationship between Scripture, tradition, and reason looks like. Scripture contains everything needed, but not everything in Scripture is needed. Everything in Scripture, however, is useful. On the one hand tradition distills what is needed and employs all that is useful, embodying both into forms of life accommodated to building up the body of believers and best equipping it to love and serve the Lord, the neighbor, and the whole creation. On the other hand, tradition should not press upon the church things contrary to Scripture or give authority to teachings or practices that it does not justify. Thus reason is a critical friend to Scripture and tradition, ensuring neither is treated as infallible, holding up a mirror to both, particularly in the face of the kingdom beyond the church, and seeking to translate both into the language and custom of the day.

Two kinds of distinctions within the notion of reason are helpful to bear in mind. One is the difference between deductive and inductive reason. Deductive logic establishes premises, or propositions, which are unambiguous statements of fact. It then sets two or more such premises

9. Stephen Sykes, *The Identity of Anglicanism* (New York: Seabury, 1978), 90.

alongside one another, and derives a conclusion by accumulating the information disclosed in the respective propositions. For example, two premises might be as follows. Miracles are very unusual; Jesus was a person who performed miracles. The conclusion would be that Jesus is a very unusual person. One may evaluate deductive logic by assessing whether each premise is true, and by checking that the conclusion genuinely arises from the premises.

By contrast, inductive logic is a process of inferring conclusions that go beyond the propositions available. Thus, unlike conclusions reached through deductive logic, which can be known for certain provided the premises are correct, conclusions reached through inductive logic can never be known for certain. For example, two premises might be: Jesus was raised after lying two nights dead in the tomb; and, there is no historical record of any event quite like this. The conclusion might be that Jesus' sayings about himself and predictions of his passion and resurrection should therefore be treated with great authority. Almost all faith statements rely on inductive reasoning of this kind. Skeptics, who reject faith as irrational, sometimes imply deductive logic is the only permissible kind. However, almost all significant aspects of life require a level of trust, and trust is precisely the quality that inclines a person to rely on the conclusions of inductive reasoning. When Episcopalians include "reason" alongside Scripture and tradition as modes of authority, they are asking that the inductive logic underlying Scripture and tradition be laid bare; the alternative is "blind faith," which expects that one should believe without the inductive process that might lead to belief being made explicit. When reason is contrasted with faith, or with revelation, the contrast usually, and unhelpfully, assumes that deductive reason is the only kind of reason in question. The debate between faith and inductive reason is altogether a more fruitful one.

A second distinction is that between theoretical and practical reason. In the simplest terms, this is the difference between truth and goodness. Theoretical reason seeks an accurate description of reality, while practical reason aspires to an excellent prescription for healthy living. Some philosophers, following Plato, have considered the two almost interchangeable; others, following Aristotle, have regarded them as two distinct but complementary fields of knowledge. Aristotle described practical reason as concerning matters which can be other than they are, whereas theoretical, or speculative, reason described matters that cannot be otherwise, but simply *are*, by necessity.

When challenges are made to Christian faith, it is helpful to make a distinction between challenges made on theoretical grounds and those made on practical grounds. For example, debates between science and religion about such issues as the beginnings of the universe, the origin of species, and the plausible historicity of the virgin birth and the resurrection, are questions of theoretical reason. Meanwhile, claims that most wars in world history have been caused or fuelled by religious difference, or that certain denominations have lost much moral credibility because of the sexual exploitation of vulnerable persons by some placed in positions of trust, are questions of practical reason. To say the Episcopal Church has been shaped by empirical and pragmatic traditions is to point to the ways its theological reasoning has tended to be more practical than theoretical in character. That is why scientific inquiry has been less troubling to most Episcopalians than to members of other traditions whose identities rest more squarely on confidence in theoretical reasoning. The overall tendency in the Episcopal Church has been to see practical and theoretical reasoning on a continuum. It does not rule out theoretical reasoning as speculative, or as contrary to Scripture and tradition, but always seek principally to establish how the truths of theoretical reason may be translated into the realities of practical existence. Perhaps the most significant way in which this emphasis is expressed is in assuming the primacy of worship as the place in which doctrine (or theoretical reason) is visualized and ethics (or practical reason) is portrayed.

The primacy of practical reason shapes the way Scripture is read and tradition is received. The Bible is not a series of metaphysical (theoretical) claims, but is primarily a story of how communities of faith have (practically) responded to the presence and activity of God in their midst. Scripture offers no account of God except in relation to such communities. Tradition is the wisdom of such communities, in the way they have continued best to understand the activity and presence of God among and beyond them, and order their lives accordingly. Thus reason is not the (theoretical) seeking of abstract first principles, as if there had not been hundreds of years of prior experience and reflection on those very things of which Scripture and tradition are the result. Instead it is the practical evaluation of how such wisdom fares in the face of contemporary challenges and scrutiny. There is no such thing as "reason alone." All reason arises out of practice and tradition of some kind, including social context, economic status, education, language, cultural norms, and much more—and for Episcopalians, reason arises out of practices and traditions from within the church.

But challenge and scrutiny are not idle friends. Reason highlights the sharp edges in Scripture and tradition. It names a history of conflict that is evident in the Bible (note the heated debate between Peter and Paul recorded in Acts 15:1–29 and Galatians 2:11–14) and occurs almost ceaselessly in the formation of tradition (note the disaffected believers who did not share the conclusions reached at the Councils of Constantinople and Chalcedon in 381 and 451 respectively). There is nothing inherently unhealthy about conflict—difference and disagreement can become sources of creativity and a refiner's fire for clarity and wisdom. Theoretical reason ensures Scripture cannot ever simply be taken uncritically for granted, while practical reason ensures tradition will never cease to be tested by the forms of life it prescribes.

A further dimension of reason that has been more prominent in recent times is the increasing attention paid to how the interpretation and reception of texts and traditions is shaped by the social locations in which they are read and practiced. What is sometimes known as the "hermeneutic of suspicion"—the inclination to mistrust the purpose and design of a text or tradition, to investigate the power relations behind or hidden in it, and to seek out and uphold the oppressed persons who are taken to be the silent casualties of the legacy—has become commonplace in many parts of the church at large, particularly in academic circles. Sometimes this means a negative tendency to regard the past as hopelessly locked into patriarchalism, racism, repression, superstition, intolerance, and much else. At other times it signifies an energizing renewal of the Episcopal Church's impulse to keep close to the ground and evaluate tradition by how it is received in its particulars.

Finally, it is essential to remember that authority has always been disputed in the Episcopal Church, and that contemporary debates about it are neither new nor especially distinctive. One helpful and succinct account of authority is provided by a report of a committee of bishops for the 1948 Lambeth Conference.[10] The report notes that "essentially Anglican" authority is dispersed rather than centralized; its many elements interact through "mutual support, mutual checking and redressing of errors or exaggerations." It possesses a "suppleness and elasticity" that "releases initiative, trains in fellowship, and evokes a free and willing obedience." (Note here a heavy emphasis on practical wisdom.) The elements of authority are "in organic relationship to each other," and the way religious experience is "ordered, mediated and verified" is likened to "the discipline of the scientific method." Scripture describes religious experience; the creeds define it; the ministry of word and sacrament mediates it; the witness of the saints and the continuing experience of the Holy Spirit (known as the *consensus fidelium*) verify it; and it is born out in episcopacy and liturgy. In other words, for Episcopalians there is no form of reasoning that is not, in the end, a form of prayer—a searching, meditating, embodied, and biblically formed encounter with the ways of God in Christ.

---

10. "The Meaning and Unity of the Anglican Communion," *The Lambeth Conference 1948*, quoted in Sykes, *Identity of Anglicanism*, 112–14.

CHAPTER 3

The Order of the Faith

Introduction: Holiness

If the first question we considered was, "What do Episcopalians believe?" and the second question was, "On what grounds do they believe it?" the third question, and the one to which this chapter responds, is, "What forms of life emerge from this belief?"

Perhaps the central scriptural statement that guides the answer to this question comes from God's words to Moses moments before the giving of the Ten Commandments on Mt. Sinai: "If you obey my voice and keep my covenant, you shall be my treasured possession out of all the peoples. Indeed, the whole earth is mine, but you shall be for me a priestly kingdom and a holy nation" (Exodus 19:5–6). A similar injunction comes from the mouth of Jesus as he utters the Sermon on the Mount: "Be perfect, therefore, as your heavenly Father is perfect" (Matthew 5:48). Holiness is about two movements: a movement apart, in order to be distinct, and a movement toward, in order to be present. Christians are made holy so that they may be a blessing to those they meet and serve. All three chapters in this section—worship, ministry, and mission—are descriptions of the forms of life that emerge from belief: and all three of these forms of life are attempts to be holy as God is holy.

Worship is the moment when human beings, on behalf of all creation, justified by the grace of Christ, stand before God through the power of the Spirit, in the presence of the angels and surrounded by the communion of saints, seeking to become what God is, holy and eternal, taking their place at the heavenly banquet, and finding their voice in the heavenly choir. Worship is people, corporately or individually, allowing God to make them holy. *Ministry* is believers opening their lives to the Holy Spirit to hear their vocation, take up roles in offering the precious gifts of the church to believers, and adopt lives of humble service in imitation of Christ, seeking to make God's life their own. *Mission* is disciples seeking to discover the holiness of God in the world while bringing the gospel to new people and places, witnessing to the kingdom of God through care for the neighbor and stranger in body, mind, and spirit, and opening the structures and institutions of society to the fruits of the Spirit.

Worship

If Episcopal faith has a central conviction, it is that doctrine and ethics, belief and practice, find their meeting place and testing ground in common prayer. If there were one symbol of the convergence of Scripture, tradition, and reason, it would be the Book of Common Prayer. In the words of one historian of spirituality in the Church of England:

> To the seventeenth—or indeed nineteenth—century layman the Prayer Book was not a shiny volume to be borrowed from a church shelf on entering and carefully replaced on leaving. It was a beloved and battered personal possession, a lifelong companion and guide, to be carried from church to kitchen, to parlour, to bedside table; equally adaptable for liturgy, personal devotion, and family prayer; the symbol of a domestic spirituality—full homely divinity.[1]

This book has gone through a number of different forms and revisions over the centuries, and the English version of 1662 and the American version of 1979 are among the several volumes that describe themselves, and are known by their users, as the Book of Common Prayer. An important part of what is distinctive about the Episcopal Church is that it focuses its identity not in an authoritative leader, nor in a declaration of faith, nor in a particular founder or style of governance, but in a pattern of prayer. The Prayer Book is the epitome of the Episcopal understanding of tradition: it is a rendering of Scripture, thoughtfully crafted, open to new insights and revisions through the experience of the faithful

1. Martin Thornton, "The Anglican Spiritual Tradition," in Richard Holloway, ed., *The Anglican Tradition* (Wilton, CT: Morehouse, 1984), 74.

over time.[2] While the particular language (especially of the 1662 Book of Common Prayer) has often been the focus of devotion and loyalty, the truer emphasis has been on the pattern itself, which we shall now outline.

The place to begin an understanding of Christian worship is in baptism. Baptism is not usually the beginning of the walk of faith. Faith more often begins in the moment or process of conversion that comes upon an adult believer, and is amplified in the course of instruction (often known as cate-chesis) that prepares the new disciple for baptism. Or it begins in the hearts of the parents of infants, who wish that their children know faith first of all as a gift of grace, cherished by familial love, and only secondarily as something to be discovered for themselves. Baptism itself embodies three distinct but overlapping processes in the body and soul of the new believer.

First there is a figurative (and sometimes actual) act of stripping, as the person to be baptized puts behind them all that stands between them and the hands of the merciful God. The imagery is of the Israelites standing on the shore of the Red Sea, with Egypt and the vengeful armies of Pharaoh behind them: the sea will devour all that oppresses, all that causes grief, sorrow, and separation between the disciple and God. But the imagery is also that of the returning prodigal son. All the inheritance that was offered to this child of God in creation is poised to be restored; all that is required is for the child to come home, for the damage done by the estrangement has been borne by the ever-loving father and is not counted against him. The stripping of the spirit is a confrontation with God's judgment and mercy; the stripping of the mind is a confrontation with God's desire to free us from slavery; and the stripping of the body is a confrontation with God's power in the face of death.

Second, there is the symbolic (or sometimes fully immersing) act of washing. The washing of new birth embodies Jesus' words to Nicodemus that we must be born of water and the Spirit (John 3:5). As the stripping is a physical enactment of death, this is a bodily enactment of resurrec-tion. There is also the washing of the mind, which echoes the words of Romans 12:2: "Do not be conformed to this world, but be transformed by the renewing of your minds, so that you may discern what is the will of God." This moment also echoes the inauguration of Jesus' ministry at his own baptism, where the heaven is open to him, the Spirit is upon him, and he is wholly embraced by the Father—this is the imagination the new disciple inherits. Yet there is also the washing—or, indeed the drowning—of the spirit, that recalls the vivid drowning of the oppres-sors in the Red Sea in Exodus and that anticipates God's final judgment on evil. All washing includes this element of drowning, the drowning of that which does not belong in the body—otherwise known as sin.

2. I am grateful to Bill Gregg for drawing my attention to this point.

The third element, more emphasized in more recent liturgies in the Anglican Communion than it had been earlier, is the clothing. Paul speaks of clothing ourselves with "compassion, kindness, humility, meekness, and patience" (Colossians 3:12). This is the activity of the church in the power of the Spirit. It is marked by activities such as anointing with oil and giving a candle, offering a commissioning prayer, and enacting a congregational welcome. This enshrines the bestowing of ministry on each new disciple, and is the focal moment of perceiving vocation. In the rite of baptism in the Episcopal Church, after the baptism itself, the priest or bishop prays that God may give the candidates "an inquiring and discerning heart, the courage to will and to persevere, a spirit to know and to love you, and the gift of joy and wonder in all your works."[3]

The Thirty-Nine Articles, ever eager to diminish Roman Catholic accretions, are keen to limit the notion of a sacrament: "There are two Sacraments ordained of Christ our Lord in the Gospel, that is to say, Baptism, and the Supper of the Lord" (Article XXV). The other five Roman Catholic sacraments—"Confirmation, Penance, Orders, Matrimony, and Extreme Unction"—are not to be so defined, "for that they have not any visible sign or ceremony ordained of God." Episcopalians have retained characteristically diverse views on the nature and number of the sacraments, but the Articles' caution is borne out by their reluctance to draw profound significance from the other five sacraments in comparison to the undisputed two. For most Episcopalians today, if not in every century before now, the central sacrament, around which liturgical and the rest of life revolves, is the eucharist.

The eucharist is centrally a shared meal, and almost always a ritual rather than a full meal. It focuses on the actions of Jesus and the disciples at the Last Supper, where Jesus took, blessed, broke, and shared the bread and later took, blessed, and shared the wine, declaring that these were his body and blood and that his disciples should henceforth do these things in remembrance of him.[4] These actions recalled the tradition of eating bread and drinking wine alongside eating bitter herbs and a lamb in the context of a Passover meal to celebrate the Jews' escape from slavery and Egypt. Jesus, in this meal and on the cross, becomes the Lamb of God, whose death ensures God passes over human sin, just as the angel of the Lord passed over the houses of the Hebrews that had the blood of the lamb on their doorposts in the days of the Pharaoh. Meanwhile, Luke portrays the Last Supper as the seventh meal (seven is the perfect Hebrew number) shared by Jesus in the gospel narrative: it thus incor-

---

3. BCP, 308.
4. See Matthew 26:26–29, Mark 14:22–25, Luke 22:15–20, and Paul's account in 1 Corinthians 11:23–26.

porates the significance of all its predecessors, notably Luke's story of the Feeding of the Five Thousand, where Jesus turns scarcity into abundance (9:12–17). The eighth meal in Luke's account is the supper on the road to Emmaus, where the disciples recognize the risen Lord in the breaking of the bread (24:30–31). Here is the paradigm for the role of the eucharist in the church, signifying the moment in which the disciples discern the continuing presence of the risen Lord. But Jesus' words, "I will never again drink of the fruit of the vine until that day when I drink it new in the kingdom of God" (Mark 14:25), point to yet a further resonance of this celebration: the great kingdom banquet that is the gospels' most prominent depiction of everlasting life with God.

Episcopalians are concerned with much more than simply recalling the circumstances of the Last Supper. Instead, they carry out together a series of actions and words that prepares them to share and receive the sacramental body and blood of Christ, and then prepares them to resume their lives, transformed by the body of Christ in all three senses of the term—Christ himself, the church, and the consecrated bread. This ordered series of actions performed by people and clergy together is known as the liturgy. (Liturgy is a generic term for ordered corporate worship, but "the liturgy" invariably means a traditional form of eucharistic worship, broadly following the Roman Catholic pattern.) The different orders, or liturgies, for the eucharist, from Thomas Cranmer's 1549 Prayer Book, through 1662 and later revisions up through today, all have slight or significant variations. But across all of them one can discern five movements.

First there is a process of gathering, in which a loose assembly (*ekklesia*, the Greek word for church, originally meant "assembly") becomes a church, a self-conscious body of Christians seeking in worship to be renewed for mission and in mission to be prepared for worship. Often there is a procession that symbolizes the church's status as a pilgrim people, having "no lasting city," journeying between Pentecost and the last day, "looking for the city that is to come" (Hebrews 13:14). Always there is a greeting, identifying the priest who is to preside over the assembly on that day and naming the presence of God. Sometimes at this point there is the Confession of Sin followed by absolution, for by beginning worship in this way, Christians are able to enter into the presence of God free from the burden of their unworthiness. Sometimes there is a song of praise, such as the ancient "Glory to God in the Highest"; and always there is a collect, a formal gathering prayer that literally "collects" all the scattered and disparate intentions of the people.

Second, the congregation discovers and rediscovers God's word in the Scripture readings. When the 1662 Prayer Book was compiled, it was assumed worshipers would already have heard the Old Testament scriptures read at Morning Prayer; thus the readings were simply a gospel passage preceded by a text from elsewhere in the New Testament. Today, especially in the Episcopal Church, but often elsewhere in the Anglican Communion, Holy Communion is the central act of worship and the Old Testament is read alongside a psalm and two New Testament scriptures. The gospel, since it records the words of Jesus, is usually given special honor by being heard standing. The sermon follows, a proclamation of the piercing word of Scripture in the context of today's church and world, and perhaps above all that moment in the church's life when Scripture, tradition, and reason meet.

Third, the people respond to the hearing of God's word. This usually includes a recitation of the Nicene Creed, the most explicit statement of the church's tradition of faith, and almost always involves intercessory prayer, called the Prayers of the People. Such prayers call on God to rend the heavens and come down, to visit once again the struggles and sufferings of God's people. Confession and absolution follow, if these did not take place earlier, and an exchange of signs of peace, recalling Jesus' words, "When you are offering your gift at the altar, if you remember that your brother or sister has something against you, leave your gift there before the altar and go; first be reconciled to your brother or sister, and then come and offer your gift" (Matthew 5:23–24).

Fourth, there is the sharing of food. Gifts of bread, wine, and money are brought to the altar, and this symbolizes the best of human efforts, rather like the five loaves and two fishes that were all that the disciples could muster at the Feeding of the Five Thousand. The priest calls on the people to lift their hearts to God and adopt an attitude of thanksgiving. In the eucharistic prayer that follows, the priest recalls the story of God's unfolding purpose through creation and covenant, before taking the bread and wine, invoking the power of the Holy Spirit on the elements and on the congregation, pronouncing Jesus' words at the Last Supper, and then calling on God, through the fruitfulness of the sacrament, to renew the church and all creation with justice and mercy. The Lord's Prayer follows and the bread is broken and distributed to the people.

Fifth, and sometimes quite briefly, the people of God are sent out for mission and ministry. The congregation offers a final thanksgiving as they are blessed and dismissed, commissioned to celebrate the eucharist they find in the world, to transform all that is a cause of distress into an occasion for thanksgiving, and to bring back to the altar the following week all that has been good and all that is in need of transformation.

What exactly takes place when the priest recalls Jesus' words (known as the Words of Institution) and invokes the transforming power of the Holy Spirit? This was the focus of much debate during the Reformation, and has remained a divisive question since. There are broadly four established understandings. The characteristic Roman Catholic view is that the bread and wine continue to look like bread and wine, but their true nature has been changed into Jesus' body and blood. Thus the worshiper truly is partaking of Christ's body. Lutherans characteristically believe that the bread and wine remain bread and wine, but that Christ, who is divine, enters believers at the moment they receive it. The Calvinist perspective is that Christ, being fully human, cannot be in more than one place at once. Christ dwells in heaven, but the bread and wine constitute a promise that the Holy Spirit will give to the disciple Christ and his "benefits" (forgiveness of sins and everlasting life) when the eucharist is shared. Finally the characteristic Zwinglian belief is that the Christian already possesses Christ, and that the words and actions at the altar are a reminder for Christians of the blessings they already enjoy.

The typical congregation in the Episcopal Church will, when canvassed, reveal a range of views across this spectrum; the Episcopal Church has never identified itself with a single position. It is simply assumed that during the prayer of thanksgiving the Holy Spirit acts upon the elements and during the receiving of communion the Holy Spirit acts within the believer. Most prayers of thanksgiving are carefully balanced to incorporate language that echoes and honors all four traditions. Thus when the priest says, "This is my body.... This is my blood," it sounds like the Roman Catholic view is being portrayed. Yet when the priest prays that the bread and wine "may be for us the body and blood of our Lord Jesus Christ" the words "for us" are a clear gesture toward the Lutheran understanding. Most prayers likewise include the language of "promise," pointing to the Calvinist perspective, and "memorial," suggesting the Zwinglian view. This ambiguity, yet relative harmony, among the four understandings of the eucharist is the most prominent of many doctrinal and ecclesial compromises made by Episcopalians. In practice the congregation's broad perspective is indicated by a number of signs that are seldom visible in the written liturgy. Thus if the table is called an "altar," and the clergy wear the white alb and richly colored stole and chasuble associated with Roman Catholic worship, and if the architecture places the events in a lofty and exalted place, these are gestures toward a more Catholic view of the proceedings at the table; if instead the term "holy table" is used, fewer, if any, formal vestments are worn, and the event is known as the Lord's Supper, these are gestures encouraging a more Zwinglian view. But these are matters on which, following the tradition of Queen Elizabeth I, the church in general has no desire to "make windows" into men's and women's souls.[5]

---

5. By this Elizabeth meant that she did not expect conformity and unanimity, but simply loyalty to her, to the nation, and to the church across a broad spectrum of theological opinion.

While the two central sacraments significantly shape worship in the Episcopal Church, they do not dominate it. Three other dimensions contribute to its general character. Thomas Cranmer, Archbishop of Canterbury at the time of Henry VIII, took five of the seven Benedictine daily offices (or regular prayers), and crafted Morning Prayer, or Matins (from the services of Matins, Lauds, and Prime), and Evening Prayer, or Evensong (from the services of Vespers and Compline). These acts of worship bookend the day for Episcopalians. They are centered on the reading of Scripture and the recitation of the psalms, and have a cherished place for scriptural and traditional canticles, the Apostles' Creed, brief responsorial prayers, and memorable collects. Over the centuries an enormous body of music has been composed for these services, and the psalm chants and canticle settings have become an important part of Anglican contributions to the universal church. Over the past fifty years the eucharist has tended to displace these offices as the most prominent congregational act of Sunday gathering. Yet for a great many Episcopalians, particularly those whose confidence in their own participation in the ministry and mission of the church is tentative but whose pursuit of holiness and the search for the mystery of God is genuine, Morning and Evening Prayer remain key dimensions of corporate worship. They embody the significance of prayer to doctrine, and the centrality of Scripture to worship.

Just as the regular rhythm of Morning and Evening Prayer orders the daily shape of time, so the liturgical calendar orders the yearly sense of season. There is a time for celebration, notably at Christmas and Easter, Ascension and Pentecost, and a time for introspection and penitence in Lent and Advent. There are saints' days to honor the church's heritage and experience the unity of the faithful living and departed. And in between there are periods of "ordinary time" to fill out the texture and breadth of Christian experience.

A further dimension of worship lies in the occasional offices, notably weddings and funerals. In keeping with the tradition of expressing faith in prayer, rather than in formal declarations, the understanding of marriage is to be found in the words said at the beginning of the marriage service. The Episcopal Church finds three purposes in marriage: mutual joy; companionship, especially in adversity; and, when and if the gift is given, the procreation of children and their nurture in the faith. Marriage is seen as established in creation, as blessed by the first miracle of Jesus at Cana in Galilee, and as offering a sign of the union between Christ and the church. The church does not marry people; they marry one another: the church simply witnesses, celebrates, seeks to meet God in Scripture, and prays for and with the couple. In blessing a marriage, the church seeks for the couple to be made holy. Thus, in a way somewhat similar to ordination, the couple is set apart, and enjoined to adopt a form of common life, in order to enrich their ministry and mission to church and world.

Likewise, funerals and memorial services are not occasions when the church does something "to" the deceased, but are for considering someone's life in the light of eternity and commending him or her to God's grace. They are times for giving thanks and proclaiming resurrection faith in the face of sadness and grief, and for offering support and strength to mourners while gently bringing the congregation face-to-face with their own mortality and degree of preparedness for it—all in the context of worshiping the living God. In almost every case the deceased's life showed and taught, intentionally or unintentionally, something of the character of God. The act of worship is a balance between what God gave in the gift of this person's life and what God gave in the gift of Christ and continues to give in the gift of the Holy Spirit. Thus such acts of worship are a prayer that the deceased's life may be safe with God and may, in its entirety, be a blessing to God's people.

All of these and many other dimensions of corporate worship both fertilize and are fertilized by the soil of personal prayer. Such prayer may follow a set liturgy, such as Morning or Evening Prayer, or it may be devotional, focusing on a passage of Scripture, a commentary or meditative reading, an icon, or the consecrated bread. It may be contemplative, beyond word or image into the heart of God, or charismatic, open to pictures or words that speak prophetically to the self or to others. It may be purposeful, eagerly interceding for a particular concern over a long period of time or repeating a short form of words over and over; it may be systematic, methodically keeping lists of causes or persons and raising each, day by day. It may follow the rhythm of a journey to work, a daily walk with a dog, or routine chores. Everything in Episcopal theology assumes and furnishes an understanding of personal prayer. Having a formal prayer book offers a model for personal devotion, just as keeping a regular rhythm of Sunday worship offers a pattern for personal faith. But there is no assumption that such personal faith should be expressed formally—only that in joy and in sorrow, in wonder and in need, at morning, noon, and night, at the dining table and in the quiet of the bedroom, the believer should turn to God in penitence, praise, thanksgiving, and expectation.

Ministry

Ministry is one of the fruits of baptism. As soon as new disciples are incorporated into the body of Christ in baptism, the gift of ministry is bestowed upon them. All ministry is Christ's ministry, so all ministry derives from being a member of Christ's body.

The church uses the terms "ministry" and "mission" in overlapping ways. Mission tends to refer to what members of the church do in relation to those who do not gather to worship, whether it takes the form of sharing faith in evangelism, sharing resources in humanitarian efforts, or building institutions and working toward transformed social structures. Meanwhile, ministry tends to refer to the ways the church orders its common life by educating its children, catechizing those new to faith, conducting its worship, managing its finances and buildings, sustaining its governance, training its clergy, overseeing its staff, and offering pastoral care. The points of overlap are considerable. Offering regular worship, for example, is part of the church's mission, but is clearly an aspect of common life; likewise most churches offer pastoral care not just to members, but to all who seek it. The simplest, but not always the most accurate, way to configure the interconnection of the two terms is that *ministry* is disciples' self-conscious participation in the church's *mission*.

Thus there are a host of activities that appropriately come under the designation of ministry. In recent years within the Episcopal Church, this greater awareness of the connection of ministry to baptism has led to a growing sense of the ministry of the whole body of Christ, often crystallized in terms such as "every member ministry." Some of these ministries, such as youth work, children's work, lay preaching and leading of worship, and eucharistic ministry to the housebound have come to involve particular training and licensing. Many other vital roles, such as financial management and the raising of funds, are not licensed, but are nonetheless integral to the flourishing of the church.

One thing that all of these activities have in common is that they are forms of the worship of God and the service of others to which the believer may expect to sense a call. Vocation is a place in the soul of the believer where creation and redemption meet: that is to say, it is a place where the manner and urgency and grace with which God redeems the world in Christ through the Holy Spirit resonates with the character, disposition, and qualities of the created person. Vocation does not simply affirm the innate gifts of the disciple; it bestows further gifts upon the disciple. Those called to ministry are not necessarily the people with the most evident or brilliant gifts, but God clothes those who are called with gifts sufficient to their task. Such vocation is seldom if ever simply an individual response to an individual word from God, for vocation emerges through communal discernment and is a reflection not just on personal potential but on fruits witnessed by others.

Among a myriad of ministries one has a particular place—not higher, but nonetheless unique. It is designated by the term "ordination." Some practices of the church, notably baptism, preaching, the pronunciation of the forgiveness of sins, blessing, and the celebration of the eucharist, are so fundamental to the life of the body that persons are set apart to care about and specialize in carrying them out faithfully and thoughtfully. There are many lay ministries that are associated with these foundational activities, such as reading Scripture, catechizing new believers, and assisting with the distribution of communion. But ordained ministry signals a distinct trust, calling, competence, training, and prayerful pursuit that these central formative practices are being administered well. From time to time that trust is jeopardized, as when a member of the clergy turns out to be living a life that falls painfully short of the community's expectations of conscience and conduct. But the validity of these core practices does not depend on the character of the person who leads them: the Holy Spirit offers treasure even through "clay jars" (2 Corinthians 4:7). In the Episcopal Church, the symbol of that trust is often the clerical collar. The collar communicates that these are persons whose theological formation, gifts in ministry, understanding of Scripture and tradition, rhythm of prayer, and transparent character make them ready, at any moment, to encounter God, in and with God's people, in joy, in despair, or in the everyday.

After the Reformation the Church of England, and subsequently the Episcopal Church, retained the threefold order of ministry—bishop, priest, and deacon. This is a significant feature of the Episcopal Church's claims to be both catholic and apostolic. The role of the deacon is variously understood in different denominations. For Episcopalians it is a unique ministry of servanthood tending to "the poor, the weak, the sick, and the lonely." Deacons are to make "Christ and his redemptive love known" by word and example, and to show "Christ's people that in serving the helpless they are serving Christ himself."[6] Traditionally those to be ordained priest are first ordained deacons, so that they become used to ordination and the community can become used to them, for a period of months or more, until the time comes for them to be ordained priest. This tradition has the disadvantage that diaconal ministry is widely seen as little more than a transitional state—the impoverishment of a rich ministry that goes back to the Acts of the Apostles. Some few, however, remain deacons permanently, affirming the servant-heartedness central to all ministry but particularly represented by this role.

The priest is an intermediary between God and the people. Martin Luther and others among the great reformers insisted that the people *as a whole* were an intermediary between God and the world—hence Luther's emphasis on the term "the priesthood of all believers." This term originates in Israel's designation in Exodus 19 as a "priestly kingdom," that is, an intermediary between God and the nations, and indeed, the whole created world. It does not mean that every believer is a priest; indeed Israel itself had representative priests, from the lineage of Aaron. These priests offered sacrifice in the temple in Jerusalem, burned incense, and mediated between God and Israel. Many Protestant denominations

6. BCP, 543.

have preferred the term "pastor" (shepherd) or "minister" (servant), often remaining suspicious of the term "priest" because it is associated with sacrifice (and are suspicious of the term "altar" for the same reason). In practice the term "priest" for Episcopalians is not centrally about the notion of a sacrifice taking place at the altar, but of the role of an intermediary between God and the people.

Is such an intermediary necessary? Christ is, after all, the "one mediator between God and humankind" (1 Timothy 2:5). Episcopalians do not believe an intermediary is strictly *necessary*; for they may commune with God in Christ through the Holy Spirit anytime, anywhere, without someone to intervene on their behalf. But they also believe priesthood is nonetheless a gracious gift of God to the church, one that focuses, refines, embodies, and unifies the people's prayers, and becomes a channel of profound blessings.

Four roles gather around the person of the priest. First, a priest represents the people to God. This is expressed liturgically in the praying of the collect, where the priest gathers together the diverse and diffuse prayers of the congregation and collects them into one, which concludes the gathering of the people before God and focuses all their attention on the source of their creation and salvation. It can also be done in the Prayers of the People, where the priest not only brings the unresolved, unexplained, and unhealed to God on behalf of the people, but also models how they are to stand before and address God. It is sometimes done in the Post-Communion Prayer and in the Collect for Purity, where well-honed words are carefully expressed to shape the way the congregation perceive its role in worship and beyond. But in recent years many, if not all, of these parts of the liturgy have come to be said jointly by priest and congregation, or, in some cases, by a single lay person. Therefore attention is focused even more on the one part the priest alone says, the prayer over the bread and wine, known as the Great Thanksgiving. Beyond the Sunday liturgy, this role is perhaps most evident when priests pray the daily office, ideally in the parish church; they are then with God, with the people on their hearts (to use a term associated with Michael Ramsey, former Archbishop of Canterbury). Whenever the priest reassures a parishioner, "You'll be in my prayers," this is the relationship that is being identified.

Second, a priest represents God to the people. When sins are forgiven, a declaration is made. This is speaking to the people for God. A sermon is preached, making the words of the scriptural text sing in the congregation's ears and dance in their hearts. This again is speaking for God. An announcement is made that the peace the people are about to share is the peace of Christ. The bread is broken and the words bring the past significance and power of Christ's death into the present reality of sharing his risen body. A blessing is given to seal the grace of God in the hearts of believers, and again these words are spoken for God to the people. And because the priest speaks such a word in the liturgy, people look to him for similar words at other times. When parents say, "How can God let my child get leukemia?" or when a farmer says, "What d'you think God is up to with this stretch of weather?" or when a mother says, "Is my son's marrying a young woman of another faith a terrible thing?" the expectation is that the priest will have something to say from a deep storehouse of wisdom, something to show for all the time spent in the presence of God, something true to the heritage of faith but fresh for the circumstances of the moment. These conversations are the heart of ministry.

These are the two core roles of the priest: speaking to God for the people and to the people for God. But churches are human institutions, too, and the priest invariably takes on two additional, ancillary roles.

One is the role one might describe as the chair. The chair's role is not to lead, but to ensure that leadership emerges, and not to decide, but to ensure a decision is taken, at the right time, by the right people, in the right way. The chair is not to dominate, but to ensure that no one and nothing dominates besides the commitment to building up the church. Without a chair, a group doesn't know how to start, what to talk about, who should speak, how to make a decision, and how to finish. The other most significant ancillary role is the role of the facilitator. This role is more playful, more like a chef composing a recipe with the ingredients that happen to be available, more given to improvisation and adept at humor, not averse to using charm, enticing people into a dance. While the chair is always focused on the final purpose of the gathering, and how most directly and appropriately to get there, the facilitator is much more focused on the gifts each person is bringing with them, and what thing of beauty might be made with those gifts that is uniquely possible with this cocktail of personalities, which would have been unimaginable without the vital permission given to each person to bring forward their gifts and let them work and play together.

The ministry that most distinctively unites Episcopal churches is that of the bishop. There is no assumption of unanimity in the church: on the contrary, the church has been, from the earliest times, in ongoing debate about the sources of its authority and the nature of its task. The bishop therefore does not seek or impose uniformity, but is to inspire loyalty from clergy and lay people and, through word and action, clarify the mission of the church in general and the diocese in particular. In the service of the ordination of a bishop in the Episcopal Church, the presiding bishop addressed the bishop-elect and declares:

A bishop in God's holy Church is called to be one with the apostles in proclaiming Christ's resurrection and interpreting the Gospel. . . .

You are called to guard the faith, unity, and discipline of the Church; and to celebrate and to provide for the administration of the sacraments of the New Covenant; to ordain priests and deacons and to join in ordaining bishops; and to be in all things a faithful pastor and wholesome example for the entire flock of Christ.

With your fellow bishops you will share in the leadership of the Church throughout the world.[7]

All bishops trace a line of authority that reaches in direct succession back to the earliest apostles. Their role is to the guard the faith, unity, and discipline of the church. While special missionary contexts might require unusual forms of proclamation, ministry, or witness, the bishop is the guardian and teacher of the faith of the apostles. Likewise, while circumstances may help to explain why prominent clergy have struggled to uphold the standards expected of them, and profound cultural influences and temptations—even a sense of call or gospel urgency—may have pushed whole congregations into graceless action, the role of the bishop is to guard the discipline of the church while exhibiting simplicity, firmness, and kindness. The presence of sin among the flock is always a disappointment, but should never be a surprise; the bishop models to the faithful what discipline and restoration look like when exercised among individuals or larger bodies of people.

More than anyone else, the bishop is the spokesperson for the church in two key areas: to the watching world and to the wider church, within the Anglican Communion and beyond. Bishops join with other bishops in leading churches across their own province and around the world. They are the physical, embodied representatives of their dioceses. This also makes them suitable figures to interact with representatives of other faiths, and recognizable persons of authority, wisdom, and integrity to address the secular world, locally and more broadly, on issues of the common good.

Mission

What are the church's hopes for the world, and how does the church perceive its role in bringing these hopes about? These are the questions of the church's mission. The church's mission is really an aspect of God's mission. In the life of the Trinity, God the Father sends the Son, and God the Father and the Son send the Spirit. Then, there is a third "sending": the Father, the Son, and the Holy Spirit send the church into the world. The sending of church to world may be considered under the broad headings of past, present, and future.

In relation to the past, the church seeks to understand, cherish, conform its life to, and—most significantly—to make known the good news of what God has done in Christ. This is the work of evangelism. There is

7. BCP, 517.

nothing inherently coercive, imperialistic, or disrespectful about evangelism. Evangelism is seeking to present the good news of God, specifically, of God's determination never to be except to be with us, and the outworking of that faithfulness in the incarnation, ministry, death, and resurrection of Jesus and the sending of the Holy Spirit. Any presentation of this message in a pressured or manipulative manner misrepresents and thus diminishes the gospel. Evangelism is appropriately conducted on many levels: individually, through personal invitation, challenge, and testimony; congregationally, through corporate initiatives to share faith through grand or humble schemes; and intercongregationally, through larger-scale programs and parachurch ministries.

With regard to the past, there is also the important work of memory. There is so much to be cherished and tenderly unearthed, so much wisdom to be celebrated, witness to be admired, sacrifice to be honored, and example to be imitated. This is especially significant in relation to those whose lives were, at the time, considered of little or no account, who because of their gender, race, class, disability, youth, or other factors were not given, in their day, the honor that was their due, but have left a legacy that speaks of goodness, truth, and beauty. This is indeed the work of mission, to search for lost coins in the household of history, coins that, gathered together, may furnish the present and future with limitless gold.

At the same time, memory is not just about cherishing, but also about challenging. Many wrongs have been done; some of these are well-known, while others were never told; some were committed in Christ's name; others, ones whose effects are felt to the present moment; others still, whose injustice is perpetuated, practiced, and even inflated today. Wrongs of the past cannot be erased; but they should not be ignored or denied. The work of mission includes the obligation to translate evil—the pervasive, insidious disease of sin that passes itself off as good—into individual sins that can be named, truthfully narrated, repented of, forgiven, and in due course healed. This process is of tremendous significance even when the perpetrators and victims themselves are long gone. For the remembering of history, its nurturing in bitterness and resentment, its transformation through truth-telling and repentance, and its healing through long struggle and profound grace, is at the heart of the gospel.

Turning to the present, the most important aspect of mission is the modeling of what God makes possible in the quality of the common life of local congregations and fellowships. If there is no practice of forgiveness, no witness of eternal life, no fruits of the Spirit, no love of God, neighbor, and self, no joy in worship, no faith, hope, or love in local community and neighborhood, there is nothing for the persuasive voice of evangelism or the plaintive cry for justice to point to. There is a place for calling on others to put their houses in order, but it requires the church to see to its own house first, and this is a crucial aspect of mission. The ability to live in peace, even with those with whom you agree, requires grace. But the ability to make a community of faith that is more than the sum of its constituent parts, from those with whom you don't instinctively agree, requires the Holy Spirit. It is a profound witness to the God who, in Christ, has broken down the dividing wall of hostility.

Committed to such humble reconciliation within its own body, the church seeks to foster and celebrate the life of the kingdom of God wherever it flourishes, and wherever it is most noticeably endangered. The irony of the kingdom of God is that its flourishing and its peril can be found in the same place, just as they were on Calvary. Much of the joy of mission is simply to share it with those who have the same reason "for the hope that is in you" (1 Peter 3:15). Often initiatives for mission and unity overlap, because there are few things that build up unity more successfully than a shared sense and practice of mission. The forging and establishing of more profound unity with Christians from different geographical, race, and class locations is an integral aspect of mission.

Jeremiah's words to the Jewish exiles in Babylon, "Seek the welfare of the city where I have sent you into exile, and pray to the Lord on its behalf, for in its welfare you will find your welfare" (Jeremiah 29:7), inspire Christians to partner with those of all faiths, and no faith, around projects and programs that enhance the good of their neighborhoods and societies. Such partnerships are goods in themselves, and not a means to any further end. Nonetheless, they build trust, help congregations know their neighborhoods better, and show the humanity of the gospel in its concern for the most ordinary aspects of created life. By participating in the mission of God, Christians seek not simply to do good, but more to make the ordinary good, and the good holy. One of the most important aspects of this ministry is peacemaking. War and armed conflict inflict death and damage upon whole populations, and the cause of peace, while of particular concern to Christians whose Lord blessed the peacemakers and taught his disciples to love their enemies, concerns the welfare of all people.

Because of oppression, misfortune, hardship, or disaster, many people around the world—Christians, those of other faiths, and those of no faith—experience poverty and other profound forms of social alienation. Here again the mission of the church is to form partnerships with those of different backgrounds, based around enabling disadvantaged people to find their own way to social healing and stability. There are significant drawbacks, however, to any form of support that never results in face-to-face contact and relies heavily on monetary gifts to third party agencies, assuming all that is required is expertise and material resources. Such intervention can underline as well as alleviate poverty in the long and short term. If the heart of the Christian faith is that God resolves to be *with* us, and only works *for* us at those times when it is needed in order to restore such companionship, any form of mission that assumes the priority of *for* over *with* can only be provisional, such as in emergency conditions. The key partners in alleviating poverty are socially disadvantaged people themselves. The parable of the Good Samaritan is not simply a mandate to attend to distress wherever and in whomever we might come upon it, however inconvenient; it is a call to recognize ourselves in the person in the ditch, and realize that the person whom God sends to save us may be someone whom everything in us resists seeing as our benefactor. Meanwhile, in the parable of the Last Judgment, Jesus points to the hungry, the thirsty, the stranger, the naked, the sick, and the prisoner as bearing his own identity, and insists that on the last day he will say, "Just as you did it to one of the least of these who are members of my family, you did it to me" (Matthew 25:31–46). This inspires Christians to expect the activity of the Spirit to be most vividly displayed in the most troubling circumstances, and seldom in those who are most conscious of their own righteousness.

The enjoyment of the common life of the church, the experience of right relationships in shared mission and fellowship, the sense of partnership in local and regional social initiatives, and the compassionate desire to be with the poor in their distress, leads to two further aspects of mission in the present tense. One is the development and practice of expert skills in key areas of human well-being. Among those, two have stood out from New Testament times to the present day: education and health. Education is not simply the fostering of faith and the cherishing of the wisdom of the ages; it is the passing-on to the poor of their most dynamic route out of poverty. The large-scale mission projects of western Christians in the nineteenth and early twentieth centuries, which sought to introduce whole populations in Africa and elsewhere to the Christian faith, were dominated by schools and hospitals. Christians are involved in education and health because, of all the places of transformation in which the Spirit is deeply invested and frequently tangible, these are the most pervasive. A vocation to be a teacher or a healthcare professional has long been regarded as among the highest callings for a Christian, and monastic communities have also been associated with these aspects of patient, skilled ministry.

The final aspect of present-focused mission arises out of reflection on the *causes* of the social ills that so much of Christian mission seeks to address. What leads people to slide into poverty? What keeps them there when everything in them longs to escape? What brings about huge disparities of wealth, miserable living conditions, constant vulnerability to violence and crime, unequal treatment under the law, undemocratic voting regulations, oppressive working relations, food shortages, chronic health problems, and high infant mortality? Such concerns are often grouped together under the term "injustice." A significant dimension of Christian mission, therefore, involves identifying the places and perpetrators of injustice, the naming of structures of oppression, the articulation of the cries of the suffering, and the campaigning, lobbying, and political deal-making involved in seeking to put things right. This is an area of compromise, not perfectionism—of pragmatic progress, not principled obstruction. The purpose is to set people free, not simply spiritually and eternally, but materially and presently. This form of mission often leads people into protest and subversion, but it can equally well lead to institution-building and legal training.

There is also a future aspect to mission. It has a particular and a general dimension. With the former, the church is called to portray in its present life the future shape of God's coming kingdom. This means entering into relationships of forgiveness and reconciliation, but also, and more poignantly, it means seeking to be present among, and offering hospitality to, those closest to Jesus' heart. These are all who have been socially excluded, whether by difference, by disadvantage, by oppression, or by their own sin. Jesus' ministry portrayed the ingathering of the exiles; so must the church's life be.

The general dimension, more pertinent in this age than ever before in the church's history, is the forging of peace not merely between humankind and God, nor even between humans one with another, but especially between humanity and the wider creation. Should human beings destroy the world, such an act would not thwart God's plans or bring creation to an end, for God is capable of restoring the world no matter how it was destroyed. Instead, Christians show their hope for the magnitude and scale of the new heavens and the new earth by the way they cherish the world in the time between the times. Mission is not saving the world, but gratefully and joyfully seeking to live and share the life of the Spirit made possible by the way God in Christ has already saved the world.

CHAPTER 4

The Character of the Faith

Introduction: Incarnation

Incarnation tells the story of what happens when the full disclosure of humanity to God meets the full disclosure of God to humanity. It is not a smooth ride, as the gospels make clear. There have been theologians and preachers ever since who have maintained that the interaction of God and humanity is, or ought to be, a straightforward matter for both parties, but it has seldom proved to be the case. Thus incarnation, perhaps the theological term most associated with the Episcopal Church, both names the inseparability of divine and human destiny and at the same time incorporates the fragility, failure, and sharp edges as well as the noble aspirations of mission through the centuries. Jesus is born in obscurity, yesterday and today; he faces danger and finds nurture, yesterday and today; he teaches, heals, and faces conflict, yesterday and today; he is betrayed and tried and crucified, yesterday and today; he is raised from the tomb and breathes his Holy Spirit on his disciples, yesterday and today.

All this we see in the three overlapping narratives that make up this chapter. The account of Anglicanism's English character attempts to distil it less into an arbitrary and constructed notion of "Englishness" than into certain key decisions, events, and movements that continue to shape the Church of England today. Next, the narrative of American dreams shows how wrong it is to see Anglicanism primarily through English eyes; few if any churches of the Anglican Communion have been less determined by the imperial imagination than the Episcopal Church, and thus few are as well placed to exhibit how Anglicanism develops its own dynamics in relation to local culture, local history, local faith, and global partners. Finally, the story of global Anglicanism offered here is inevitably incomplete in scope, not just in detail: key areas such as Latin America, the Middle East, and the Far East are overlooked altogether. I have sought to give an account that emphasizes the role of local evangelists without playing into the assumption that the growth of churches always followed the contours of the British Empire and the initiative of daring British missionary entrepreneurs.[1] One consequence of this is that my account tries to acknowledge honestly the sense of lament that must accompany a truthful telling of the story of much Christian missionary activity, notwithstanding the brave individuals who went against the grain and spoke up for a deep engagement with and respect for local cultures and leadership. It is not for nothing that a leading British theologian seeks for the Church of England to become a "pioneeringly honest ex-oppressor church."[2] It is not for nothing, also, that this account concludes with Ireland, one land that as much as any other has reason to wonder whether Anglican witness in its midst has, overall, constituted a blessing.

English Legacies

I shall attempt to characterize the distinctive features of English Anglicanism by identifying a number of key dates and elucidating their significance.

The first date is 664, the year the Synod of Whitby (near York, on the English northeast coast) convened representatives of the Celtic and Roman traditions. The Celts had brought Christianity from Ireland via the Scottish island of Iona and the Northumbrian island of Lindisfarne. The Romans traced their heritage to Pope Gregory the Great and his sending of Augustine of Canterbury in 597 to convert the English. The pretext for the synod was to come to a common mind on the manner of establishing the date of Easter, and the victory of the Roman party marks a symbolic, decisive, and largely permanent shift in English Christianity from

---

1. In this account I have deliberately followed the ethos and work of Kevin Ward, *A History of Global Anglicanism* (Cambridge: Cambridge University Press, 2006), on which this account is closely based.

2. Andrew Shanks, "Honesty," in *Praying for England,* ed. Samuel Wells and Sarah Coakley (New York: Continuum, 2008), 125–46.

Celtic to Roman dominance. Put differently, England was and is part of Europe, culturally and religiously, rather than primarily part of an island (or group of islands) unto itself, and yet it is not as wedded to Europe as most of its continental neighbors. The Church of England is the same. It is part of Catholic Christianity, part of the Reformation heritage; and yet it has significant local character, Celtic and otherwise, that makes it unique.

A second date is 1075, the year when Pope Gregory VII overhauled the parish system throughout Europe. Theodore of Tarsus, Archbishop of Canterbury in the seventh century, largely adopted the existing Anglo-Saxon township structure in which minster churches in the towns served the countryside around them, until landowners oversaw the construction of smaller churches whose parishes largely coincided with the boundaries of their own estates. Each parish, at least in theory, had its own priest. The role of the parish priest was renewed in the tenth century by Dunstan, also Archbishop of Canterbury, who enhanced both the clergy's education and their role in promoting the well-being of all who resided in their parish. Pope Gregory VII's reforms, furthermore, brought the English parish system into line with that of most of Europe.

It is hard to overestimate the significance of the parish for the imagination of English Anglicanism. The parish embodies the Church of England's commitment to the flourishing of every resident of the land, and demonstrates (in the way the priest shares the life of the people) that God cares about what they care about, thereby embodying God's love for humanity in minute particulars and the everyday rhythms of life. This is how the Church of England expresses its care for place, and for the poor; this is its essential ministry of presence and its commitment to seek God in the ordinary and abiding, the fragile, the contingent, and the tragic. The economics of being so tied to the landed classes, however, has sometimes meant the church has come adrift from the poor and thus been slow to respond to urbanization both materially and imaginatively; these are the weaknesses of its strengths.

A third date is 1559. The English Reformation was about governance and faith, but it was not always about both. Thus for King Henry VIII, England was an empire that had no need to be subject to the Pope, but was directly under God's own decree, as was legislated in 1534. Henry had no desire to make innovations in doctrine or to alter the Catholic faith. By contrast his chief minister, Thomas Cromwell, was inspired by Martin Luther and sought to introduce the new Protestant perspective under the guise of reforming the church's governance. Likewise Thomas Cranmer, Archbishop of Canterbury, set about revising the church's liturgy in line with Reformed notions of priesthood and sacraments, as represented in his Prayer Books of 1549 and 1552. For the Roman Catholic Queen Mary, who ruled from 1553 to 1558, governance and faith went together and both required obedience to Rome. On Queen Mary's death,

Queen Elizabeth restored English governance, while seeking a balance between Catholic order and Reformed faith—such a compromise constituted the Elizabethan Settlement of 1559. Henceforth a wide diversity of theological convictions have found their authority in this story of origins, and the Church of England has never been well placed to take the high ground as regards freedom from state interference. The Settlement made English Anglicanism an almost unique middle way, or *via media*, between Catholic and Reformed faith, and this is part of its inherent character.

The next date, 1662, is the only one that has become almost a proper name. It is the date of the publication of the Book of Common Prayer, which has been used in most churches in the Anglican Communion at least until the 1920s and in many cases to this day. The English Civil War of the mid-seventeenth century, followed by the Commonwealth and Protectorate, brought to the surface numerous groups, notably Presbyterians, Independents (later Congregationalists), and Baptists, as well as more radical groups such as the Quakers. The Restoration, in which Charles II was brought to the throne in 1660, restored also a church and liturgy much more in line with the 1552 Prayer Book, setting aside Reformed order and worship. The Book of Common Prayer characterizes English Anglicanism at least as much as the parish system. It shows that the church's identity lies in prayer rather than in doctrinal structure or declaration, and affirms that public prayer is the definitive form. Such prayer is "common"—in other words, not primarily for the "religious" but held in common by all. Moreover it assumes that such prayer is founded on the written word, rather than the extempore spirit, being inscribed on the heart by habit and repetition.

Yet 1689 represents the limits of the vision of 1662. When King James II looked certain to restore Catholicism in England, he was deposed by a united Protestant front in 1688. While the events of 1660 had shown that England would not become wholly Protestant, 1688 had shown that neither would it become Catholic. But the dissenting Protestants were not going to go away, and with the Act of Toleration of 1689 they were allowed to worship legally in their own places of worship and with their own ministers. (In 1828 they were given full rights, a freedom extended to Catholics in 1829.) The notion of the Church of England as the church for all the English thus failed, and the Church of England became, in reality if not in its own imagination, one denomination among others. The Oxford Movement, an engine of Catholic renewal in the Church of England, began when it became clear that the nation's church, governed by Parliament, was now, in its doctrine and order, being overseen partly by dissenters and Catholics. It was at this point that the identity of Anglicanism—a term first used around this time—became identified less with Englishness and more with specific liturgical, doctrinal, and historical commitments, such as more frequent Holy Communion and the introduction of vestments in worship, almost all of which were (and are) deeply contested.

The date 1867 marks a more significant reason why Anglicanism could no longer simply be identified with Englishness: it had become a loose federation of churches, most of which had strong links to the English Reformation. These included the American Episcopal Church, the Scottish Episcopal Church, which departed from the Presbyterian Church of Scotland in 1582, and the churches shaped significantly by British colonial expansion, including Canada, India, Australia, and the West Indies. All of these began to take on an identity influenced, but not dominated, by the Church of England. One key date in this process is 1799, which marked the founding of the Church Missionary Society (CMS). The Church of England failed to incorporate the Evangelical Revival of the eighteenth century, most notably Methodism, within its structures, but one result was the impetus that evangelicals like English politician William Wilberforce gave to overseas missions. Thus CMS began with three goals: abolition of the slave trade, social reform at home, and world evangelization. Its great leader from 1841 to 1872, Henry Venn, coined the "three-self principle" for overseas churches: self-government, self-propagation, and self-finance. In 1867 Archbishop of Canterbury Charles Longley convened the first Lambeth Conference of Anglican bishops, and 76 of the 144 bishops attended.[3] Thirteen further conferences, around every ten years, have been called since. A distinct style of leadership has emerged. The Archbishop of Canterbury convenes the conferences but has no official authority beyond England, while the conference resolutions are not decrees, but guides to future action. Provinces within the Communion are tied together by bonds of affection rather than obligation.

In a very different vein, 1870 brought the Education Act of Prime Minister William Gladstone's reforming Liberal government. Prior to this, education had been largely in the hands of the churches, especially the Church of England. Henceforth the government funded schools where they did not previously exist, in a decisive move toward universal education. Education still remains, to a degree unthinkable in the United States with its separation of church and state, profoundly influenced by the church, with a daily act of worship prescribed by law (if not always honored in practice) in every school. There still remains, in many parts of England, an assumption that if children are to discover the Christian faith, they may be expected to do so in school. There are nearly seven thousand state-funded faith schools in England today, most of them overseen by the Church of England. Education has long been the principal frontier of the Church of England's mission.

3. Of the 76 bishops who attended, 18 were from England, 5 from Ireland, 6 from Scotland, 28 were "colonial and missionary" bishops, and 19 were from the United States (http://www.lambethconference.org/resolutions/).

The twentieth century marks the era when active church participation became a minority pursuit. Three dates perhaps summarize this period. The first is 1941. William Temple, along with George Bell and Michael Ramsey, was one of the most remarkable church figures of the period. In 1941, Temple convened the Malvern Conference, attended by 400 priests and lay people, with speakers including T. S. Eliot and Dorothy L. Sayers. It was the darkest hour of the war, but Temple was already envisaging a country fit for victorious soldiers to return to. The Labour government of 1945–51, with its wide-ranging welfare reforms, owed a great deal in its vision and imagination to Temple and the conversations he ignited. More than anyone else, Temple embodied the Church of England's commitment to social ethics and its willingness to seek the common good while closely concerned for the poor. (The *Faith in the City* report of 1985, calling attention to the plight of deprived inner- and outer-urban areas, lies squarely in this tradition.) But the welfare reforms of the postwar period marked the takeover by the state of many of the social roles hitherto performed by the church, and thus, while building up the kingdom of God, hastened the decline of the church.

The next significant date is 1964, when John Robinson, the Bishop of Woolwich in South London, published *Honest to God*, an attempt to popularize liberal postwar theological movements in an effort to make Christianity comprehensible to a secular age. It sold a million copies in ten years. While promoting the fresh air of honest theology, it was more memorable for the traditional affirmations it undermined than for the newer convictions it advocated. *Honest to God* epitomized the wind of change sweeping church and society, and one indicative statistic is that Church of England ordinations fell from 636 in 1963 to 273 in 1976, a precipitous decline.[4] Believing is clearly not identical to or even fundamentally characteristic of belonging. Nonetheless, the "*Honest to God* debate" identifies a secular confidence, a sense that the world was comprehensible without recourse to faith (or at least to the church) that remains highly significant in English culture, and that found its high watermark in the 1960s.

Another important date is 1967. In this year one thousand Church of England evangelicals, led by John Stott, the long-time rector of All Souls, Langham Place in London, met at Keele in Staffordshire. Prior to Keele, in the words of one prominent evangelical scholar, evangelicals in England were associated with "archaic theology, spiritual conceit, ecclesiastical isolationism, social unconcern, pessimism about the world and the Church, an old-fashioned lifestyle, and a cultural philistinism."[5]

---

4. Adrian Hastings, *A History of English Christianity 1920–2000* (London: SCM Press, 2001), 552.

5. James Packer, quoted in Hastings, *History of English Christianity,* 553.

After Keele, evangelicals entered conversations about poverty, liturgy, ecumenism, and, perhaps most of all, about the eucharist. The result is that today, having entered and invigorated the structures and moved out of the shadows, evangelicals make up the most vibrant, most engaged, and most populous dimension of the newly ordained, the regular worshipers, and the financial supporters of the Church of England.

Women were finally admitted to the priesthood in 1994. They had been formally admitted as deaconesses since 1869, as readers since 1969, and as deacons since 1987. Yet in order to pass this legislation through General Synod (the Church of England's legislative body), a system of alternative episcopal oversight had to be established, recognizing the "two integrities" of those who did and those who did not endorse women as priests. Not only did this move inaugurate a period of considerable complexity, more acutely felt in some dioceses than others, but also set a precedent that was bound to be exploited when the General Synod initiated a draft law allowing women bishops in 2010. Furthermore, it ushered in an era of multiple ecclesial realities that started to become even more elaborate once the global controversy over the ordination of noncelibate gays and lesbians began in earnest. The Church of England has prided itself on being one large tent. It is not clear, however, whether it can continue so to describe itself as that "tent" becomes increasingly divided, with fewer flaps linking the respective sections together.

American Dreams

Christians often assume that they know what Judaism is—Christianity with the New Testament removed. Thus they invariably ignore the enormously significant developments in Judaism since the time of Christ and have a hugely impoverished understanding of Judaism. A similar dynamic tends to be at work in the English Anglican's view of the Episcopal Church, which is to assume the Episcopal Church is simply the Church of England without the monarch at its head and bishops in the House of Lords. But in reality the Episcopal Church, from its very beginnings, has greatly differed in form and conviction from the Church of England.

One of its distinctive features has been the significant role played by the laity at every stage in its development. For example, there was no bishop until the consecration of Samuel Seabury by bishops of the Scottish Episcopal Church in 1784. Thus for well over 150 years, since the first missionary clergy were sent to Virginia, the congregations depended on a mixture of overseas funding, lay stewardship, and, in North and South Carolina, Maryland, Virginia, Georgia, and New York City, funding from the government as the established church. Nonetheless, many of these congregations had no clergy for lengthy periods and much of the provision of worship came about through lay initiative. The overseas funding largely derived from the London-based Society for the Propagation of the Gospel in Foreign Parts. (When the War of Independence began in 1776, the stronger parishes tended to side with the patriots and the weaker parishes, more dependent on English support, tended to be loyalists.[6]) The seventeenth- and eighteenth-century Episcopal Church was primarily a lay movement, and this long history of lay leadership equipped it well for the turbulent times after independence, and is still significant today.

The American Revolution was a catastrophe for the Church of England in the former colonies, and once the era had passed and new arrangements were in place, American Episcopalians faced a struggle not only to form a new identity but to secure their very survival. While it may be difficult to perceive from a twenty-first-century perspective, the Revolutionary War seemed to some in the Church of England to be uncomfortably reminiscent of the English Civil War of the 1640s. Puritan refugees from seventeenth-century Anglican domination in England had shaped the culture of New England, and even though several signatories of the Declaration of Independence were Anglican laymen, many Anglicans in America and England saw the revolution as a Puritan revolt. And this perception is not entirely an eighteenth-century relic. The notion that the monarchy and the excessive authority of bishops constitute forms of oppression of which Americans still do well to be wary, is a view that is still heard in Episcopal Church circles to this day.

The post-Revolutionary disestablishment of religion shook the Church of England in the former colonies to its core. Quickly the newly birthed Protestant Episcopal Church had to find new ways of financing itself. It also had to adjust to a resident episcopacy, having not previously had its own bishops, and it had to compete in a religious marketplace. The emphasis on lay leadership served the church well in this new context. The role of the laity is born out in the governance of the Episcopal Church. Its first General Convention took place in 1785, and its constitution drew on an underlying Presbyterian ethos and also sought to balance interests that might otherwise conflict, which reflected republican assumptions. Originally there was one House of Deputies, made up of clergy and laity; in due course a House of Bishops was added, yet with no conclusive power of veto. The Episcopal Church tends to have a confidence in its constitutional arrangements comparable to the confidence of the nation as a whole in the serviceability, sufficiency, adaptability, and unique virtues of its own constitution. There is, accordingly, no

6. See David Hein and Gardiner H. Shattuck Jr., *The Episcopalians* (New York: Church Publishing, 2006), 38.

question that the date 1791 marks a profound difference between the identity of the Episcopal Church and that of the Church of England. The First Amendment to the Constitution, passed in that year, begins with the words, "Congress shall make no law respecting an establishment of religion, or prohibiting the free exercise thereof." Thus there is no governmental role in advancing or inhibiting religious practice. In more recent years this has been understood as not just a federal proviso but one restricting all levels of government.

It might be thought that the Civil War of 1861–65 would be at least as devastating for the Episcopal Church as the Revolutionary War had been. A precedent was set when the dioceses within the Confederacy created their own, separate Protestant Episcopal Church in the Confederate States of America. (The Episcopal bishops of Louisiana and Georgia were two of the largest slaveholders in the country.) The division of the state required, it seemed, the division of the church. The relative silence of church leaders in the midst of the crisis may seem disturbing today: the Boston preacher and hymn-writer Phillips Brooks commented that Episcopalians seemed unsure "whether there was a war going on or not, and whether if there was it would be safe for them to say so."[7] Yet this quietism in the pulpit contributed to an atmosphere whereby reconciliation of the two churches followed not much more than six months after the conclusion of such a devastating and divisive war. Nonetheless, it was only eight years later, in 1873, that the church split again—this time over ritualism. Some more evangelical members found the Catholic liturgical tendencies, arising from the Oxford Movement in England in the 1830s and 40s, unacceptable, and established the Reformed Episcopal Church, which as late as 2009 reported over 13,000 members.

A particular characteristic of the Episcopal Church is that, while outsiders tend to associate it with an upper-middle class cultural ethos, it nonetheless sees itself as closely concerned with issues of social justice. This paradox has long been the case. Before the Civil War, African Americans had been members of the Episcopal Church in significant numbers, albeit in many if not most cases, as slaves rather than by their own choice. After the war, Episcopalians engaged in a long and substantive debate about appropriate ways to do ministry with and for the freed slaves, many of whom were church members. Unlike, for example, the Methodists, the Episcopal Church never formally split along race lines; yet it expended considerable efforts to create separate arrangements and institutions that in the end kept African Americans subordinate. These efforts included the founding of a segregated black seminary at Petersburg, Virginia, in 1878, and the consecration of two black bishops, Edward Demby and Henry Delany, to work specifically among African Americans. (It was the emergence of the Jim Crow laws, especially around the time of the First World War, that gave segregation the roots and form that make it such a painful memory today.) From the 1950s such provisions began to unravel: for example, a resolution at the 1952 General Convention forbade seminaries or colleges from using race as a pretext for excluding certain students, and in 1954 the diocese of South Carolina welcomed three black parishes into its convention. The lawyer Pauli Murray, later to become the first African American woman ordained in the Episcopal Church, played a major role in the lead-up to the landmark 1954 *Brown vs Board of Education* decision on school segregation.

The role of Native Americans in the Episcopal Church has seldom received the same level of either contrition or attention. This is a story with many signs of hope, with significant presence and ministry in Oklahoma, Milwaukee, and Minneapolis, among other places.[8]

The Episcopal Church's sense of its own unique role in society was expressed in two late-nineteenth-century initiatives that have significant parallels with contemporary developments in England and have abiding resonances to this day. The first was the annual gathering known as the Church Congress that first met in 1874 and considered the major issues of the day. These congresses offered a forum for the sharing of a wide range of theological opinions, one factor that contributed to the Episcopal Church's being able to navigate controversies, such as the science-religion debate over evolution, more equably than some other denominations. They also established the Episcopal Church's concern for the transformation taking place as the United States became an industrial society, concerns that gave rise to the Social Gospel movement and were eloquently expressed by the Episcopalian laywoman Vida Dutton Scudder. This attention also led to the setting apart by the Bishop of Maryland of five women in 1857 as the church's first deaconesses (an order officially recognized in 1889), and to the prevalence of social outreach ministries among downtown churches. Here the prominence of the incarnation, so much associated with late-Victorian English Anglicanism, found deep roots in Episcopal Church soil. A second wave of incarnational ministry, in which affluent Episcopalians set out to live in poor urban neighborhoods, came about in a number of northeastern cities in the 1950s.

The second development was the growth of the national church ideal. Christianity was becoming increasingly associated with American identity, and perceived, along with democratic civilization and education, as part of the unique gift of the United States to the world. The building of the National Cathedral (an Episcopal foundation) in Washington, D.C.,

8. Ward, *History of Global Anglicanism*, 62–63.

which began in 1907, is the most striking symbol of the Episcopal Church's conviction that it was America's natural national church. Another aspect of this conviction was the assertion of the Chicago-Lambeth Quadrilateral, first proposed by William Reed Huntingdon in 1870, and adopted by the Episcopal House of Bishops at the 1886 General Convention in Chicago.[9] This sense of confidence was matched by the Episcopal Church's tripling in size from nearly 350,000 to over one million members from 1880–1920 (rising to 3.3 million by 1960).[10] Meanwhile, its commitment to and success in spearheading ecumenical relationships resulted in the Bishop of the Philippines, Charles Brent, being invited to chair the first World Conference on Faith and Order at Lausanne, Switzerland, in 1927; however, attempts in the 1930s and 1940s to unite with the Presbyterian Church failed. The same conviction about having a broad responsibility without being an established church lay behind the role played by the Episcopal Church in laying down institutional foundations for the Anglican Communion, notably the founding of the Anglican Consultative Council in 1969. Those who have criticized the Episcopal Church in recent years for stretching the bonds of communion have perhaps at times forgotten how much it did to forge them in the first place.

Episcopalians found themselves profoundly divided by the turbulent social movements of the 1960s. It is arguable that the church remains divided between those who continue to see these movements—in relation to race, war, gender, and, by extension, sexuality—as definitive, and those who do not. The contrast is well expressed in the succession of Presiding Bishops. John Hines, who was elected in 1965, sought to locate Episcopalians on the side of the dispossessed and oppressed peoples of the nation. His successor in 1974, John Allin, while he considered himself a liberal by Mississippi standards, opposed the ordination of women and had an altogether different set of concerns from his predecessor. These differences were reflected in the Episcopal Church more broadly. For some, an unjust law was no law at all; for others, civil disobedience was a polite name for lawlessness. For some, Christ came to save the world, and political action was all of a piece with worship, pastoral care, and evangelism; for others, politics was a dangerous distraction from the true work of the church.

The circumstances of the first ordination of women to the priesthood are especially significant for the self-understanding of the Episcopal Church. Proposals had narrowly failed at the General Conventions of 1970 and 1973; those who saw the question as one of civil rights were

9. Huntingdon saw one of the Episcopal Church's key advantages as a truly national church lying in the fact that, unlike Roman Catholicism, it was ethnically pure. See Hein and Shattuck, *Episcopalians,* 89.

10. Hein and Shattuck, *Episcopalians,* 112, 119.

eager to stage some kind of direct action to bring the church to its senses. Thus it was that two retired bishops, together with one who had recently resigned from his diocesan position, acting contrary to the will of the local bishop, ordained eleven women before a congregation of two thousand in Philadelphia in July 1974. A year later another retired bishop ordained four more women to the priesthood in Washington, D.C. The House of Bishops expressed profound misgivings. It seemed to many that procedure, authority, and discipline were in open conflict with love and justice. In 1976 ordination to the priesthood was opened to women; by 1979 there were almost 300 women in ordained ministry; and the first woman bishop was ordained in 1989.

Given the increasingly polarized character of the Episcopal Church—one way in which the church has reflected the dynamics within American society—it is remarkable and admirable how broad a consensus has formed around the 1979 Book of Common Prayer. In the Church of England it has long been common for Anglo-Catholics to incorporate elements of the Roman missal, and for Anglican evangelicals to take pride in making their worship "nonliturgical," often to make worship more "seeker-friendly" and thus more fitted to evangelism. By contrast in the Episcopal Church, the use of a written and shared liturgy is a significant and striking point of unity across the theological spectrum. Within the 1979 Prayer Book, one line is cited perhaps more than any other in current debates of faith and order. It is the final question of the eight parts of the Baptismal Covenant: "Will you strive for justice and peace among all people, and respect the dignity of every human being?"[11] For some in the contemporary Episcopal Church, these words have attained the force of Martin Luther's famous words, "Here I stand; I can do no other."

To understand the contemporary controversy over homosexuality, it is essential to recognize that the debate arose in a context where the Episcopal Church had already long (at least since the 1960s) been committed to a trajectory that defined itself by what the Baptismal Covenant calls "respect for the dignity of every human being." As one observer puts it, "The Anglican church worldwide can no more contrive permanently to marginalize homosexual people or remove them from its fellowship than it could continue to accept slavery, the inferiority of women, or the natural superiority of European civilization."[12] Meanwhile, there had always been vocal elements in the Episcopal Church that believed that such social causes were a distraction from the central call to worship, discipleship, and evangelism, or, that because acceptance of gay and lesbian relationships seemed to

11. BCP, 305.
12. Ward, *History of Global Anglicanism*, 315. Much of the following section has been drawn from this work.

contravene Scripture, to ordain them as priests and bishops constituted an unacceptable doctrinal departure. After the 1998 Lambeth Conference, it became clear that the wider Anglican Communion was going to regard American decisions on these matters as having global ramifications. Clergy and lay people within the Episcopal Church who opposed what now seemed the almost inevitable movement toward the formal recognition of the legitimacy of gay and lesbian relationships were looking to secure the oversight of bishops from the global South, a strategy that cut them off from local episcopal structures. Thus the ordination of a partnered gay man, Gene Robinson, as Bishop of New Hampshire in 2003, was not a watershed moment, but one step in a long-term realignment of those with diverging but previously reconcilable understandings of faith and mission.

Global Dimensions

The global Anglican Communion defies generalization. While I very much hope that the vast majority of the eighty million members of the Anglican Communion worldwide would subscribe to the description of the faith I have offered in this book, there is not a great deal else that would be shared by almost every member of the global church. Only sixteen of its thirty-eight provinces use the term "Anglican" in their church's name. The Scots, Americans, Filipinos, and Sudanese, for example, use the term "Episcopal," while the term "the Church of . . . " is used in England, Ireland, Pakistan, Nigeria, and Uganda. There are also other distinctive names such as "the Church in Wales" and "the Anglican Episcopal Church in Japan." Most provinces have developed their own indigenous liturgies as well. It is no longer the case, furthermore, that every church sends its bishops to the decennial Lambeth Conference. In what follows, therefore, I can only aspire to offer some sense of this considerable diversity.

There can be no doubt that the heartland of the Anglican Communion today lies in Africa. Britain abolished the slave trade in 1807, but British participation in the transportation of around ten to fifteen million people from West Africa across the Atlantic over the preceding three hundred years is not a legacy easily dispelled. Many former slaves (known as "re-captives," and their descendants as Creoles) returned in the early 1800s to West Africa, where their relations with indigenous tribes remained complex. For a great number of them, Christianity seemed to be the source of their freedom, and Anglican practices took root, especially in Sierra Leone. One freed slave was Samuel Ajayi Crowther, who was born in 1806 in what is now northern Nigeria, was enslaved in 1821, and was soon released by the British. He was baptized in 1826, was ordained in 1843, translated the Bible into Yoruba, and was ordained bishop in 1864. Crowther was a key figure in blending indigenous cultures with the practices of Christianity. The white missionaries, however, struggled to entrust church leadership to local people—there was not another African-born diocesan bishop until the 1950s—even though the missionary work was largely conducted by local pastors and evangelists.

While the size of the churches, particularly in Nigeria, increased dramatically, there remained two unresolved tensions: first, Anglicanism's ability to adapt itself to local customs and accommodate local notions of marriage, healing, and spiritual forces; and second, the encounter with the rapidly expanding presence of Islam. The Church of Nigeria today is vibrant: it has an estimated twenty million members, around one hundred dioceses, a vigorous campaign of evangelism in the largely Muslim north, a strong attachment to the 1662 Book of Common Prayer, significant charismatic influences, and a decidedly conservative stance on issues of sexuality and women's ministry.

While Anglicanism came later to East Africa than to West Africa, the former has become the second major area of its flourishing today. Uganda has around nine million Anglicans, with Tanzania and Kenya numbering a further four million between them. The persecution of Christians by the Kabaka in 1885–87, in which many local Anglicans and Roman Catholics, together with the Bishop of Eastern Equatorial Africa, James Hannington, were executed, still lives in the Ugandan church's memory. The first Ugandans were ordained in 1893 and Alfred Tucker became the first Bishop of Uganda in 1897. In 1913 Bishop Tucker Theological College (today Uganda Christian University) was founded in Mukono.

The success of Anglican evangelism in Uganda relied upon military force to subdue the Kabaka and keep the Muslims in check. British missionaries in turn prioritized the conversion of the cultural elites and the education of their children; the poorer classes tended to become Roman Catholics, although the Anglican bush schools were widespread and effective. A major step toward freeing the Anglican Church in Uganda (known now simply as "Church of Uganda") from colonial constraints was the East African revival, which began in Rwanda in 1935, and deeply affected Uganda, Tanganyika (as Tanzania was then known), and Kenya. It preached a radical gospel of equality between black and white, strong antipaganism, strict monogamy, and piercing honesty. In all it was a reassertion of a new communal African identity, and its influence has only been surpassed in recent years by the widespread Pentecostal movement. Uganda experienced a second era of martyrdom during the rule of Idi Amin, including the killing of Archbishop Janani Luwum in 1977. Both before and after Amin's regime, Anglicans were closely associated with the Uganda People's Congress, but Yoweri Museveni, president since 1986, has defused much sectarian tension. The long-running insurgency of the Lord's Resistance Army in the north of the country has meanwhile helped to unite the churches in a common cause. The Anglican Church of Uganda has also been a leader in responding to the AIDS crisis in East Africa. In addition, it has played a controversial role in the American church; since Uganda regards itself in full communion with the Anglican Church in North America, this has caused deep tensions to exist between it and the Episcopal Church.

The Episcopal Church of the Sudan claims five million members. It traces its history independently of the East African provinces, being more closely related to the churches of the Middle East. The key figure was Archibald Shaw, who adapted the Christian faith to the culture of the nomadic Dinka people in southern Sudan, and brought to ordination the first Sudanese bishop, Daniel Deng Atong, in 1955. The East Africa revival was influential in many parts of southern Sudan, and the Zande people took more readily to the faith than the Dinka had. Independence in 1956 sparked an almost continuous civil war between the Arab north and the Christian and animist south, which only concluded in 2005, with independence for the south following in 2011. Much suffering resulted from the long and relentless war: consequently Sudan epitomizes the suffering church within the Anglican Communion.

It is impossible to tell the story of the Anglican Church of Southern Africa (which has 2.5 million members in South Africa and perhaps another million in nearby states) without recognizing the complexity of the colonial and apartheid eras. The first Bishop of Cape Town, Robert Gray, was appointed in 1848, not long after the end of slavery ten years earlier. He established the principle of a church that included all races, a principle considerably ahead of its time and often breached, but nonetheless significant. He appointed John Colenso as Bishop of Natal in 1852. Colenso learned the Zulu language and painstakingly sought to redefine doctrines of sin and justification to adapt to local culture and inherited wisdom. He also embraced the new "historical-critical method" of biblical criticism, which was considered a radical move at the time. As a result Gray tried Colenso as a heretic in 1863, but the latter claimed Gray had no jurisdiction over him and won his case, remaining bishop until his death in 1883 and advocating for the Zulu cause. (The widespread disquiet about the case was a significant pretext for the calling of the first Lambeth Conference in 1867.) In the lead-up to and aftermath of the 1899–1902 Boer War, anxieties over how Anglicans related to the Afrikaner population distracted attention from the blatant injustices being perpetuated toward the nonwhite communities, particularly in relation to land and voting rights. From 1948, the victory of the National Party regularized and formalized segregation under the policies of apartheid. Alan Paton was a white Anglican who voiced theological objections in the 1940s, while Ambrose Reeves and Trevor Huddleston were among those who spoke out in the 1950s; Gonville ffrench-Beytagh and Hannah

Stanton continued this prophetic stance in the 1960s. The government continued to dismiss the Anglican Church as the continuation of outdated British colonialism, and the Anglican Church unfortunately failed to make the gestures and statements that would disprove this.

The key representative of a very different kind of Anglicanism was Steve Biko, a Xhosa medical student who founded the Black Consciousness Movement and was involved in the World Student Christian Federation. He was beaten to death in police custody in 1977. Another key figure was Desmond Tutu. General Secretary of the South African Council of Churches in 1978 and Archbishop of Cape Town in 1986, Tutu was the visible representative of the spirit of the Kairos Document, which put forth a prophetic theology in place of church (Anglo) and state (Afrikaner) theology. Tutu's role in the Truth and Reconciliation Commission that followed the end of apartheid, moreover, is perhaps the most significant political contribution of an Anglican cleric anywhere in the world today. Nonetheless, South African Anglicanism, somewhat like the Episcopal Church, has become so politicized that many have wondered if it still has a place for them. Meanwhile, many Africans still see Anglicanism as less indigenous than, for example, the Pentecostal churches.

The Church of South India (CSI) and The Church of North India (CNI) represent two major ecumenical endeavors. In India, unlike Africa, the Church of England sought to serve the needs of the European population and not to disturb the religious ecology of the native peoples. Gradually in the 1800s evangelical missionary work was permitted and dioceses were created, but by the 1900s Indian nationalist sentiment was becoming cause for concern. Thus only one Indian, Samuel Azariah, was made a bishop in the whole of the colonial era. In general the missionary approach was to convert the elites without dwelling extensively with the poorer classes. Negotiations to form a union of the Anglican, Methodist, and Reformed churches in South India began in 1919 and culminated in the formation of the Church of South India in 1947, a month after Indian independence. Many English Anglicans, including T. S. Eliot, were deeply troubled about the infringements on episcopal order that seemed inevitable in an ecumenical polity, and the CSI had to wait until 1998 for its full recognition in the Anglican Communion. Yet it has thrived because of, rather than in spite of, the extent of its ecclesial diversity. While outstanding missionary bishops included Lesslie Newbigin, the church has from the start been very largely Indian in character and leadership. The churches in North India were weaker and their ecclesial structure disrupted by the creation of first Pakistan in 1947 and then Bangladesh in 1971. Nonetheless, the Church of North India came into being in 1970, including, unlike its southern counterpart, Lutherans, Baptists, and Disciples of Christ. The two Indian churches have a combined membership of over five million.

Oceania remains one of the most numerically significant Anglican regions. Over 70 percent of Oceanic dwellers are Christian, and Anglicans make up around 18 percent of the population.[13] The Anglican Church of Australia has around 3.7 million members, making it larger than the Episcopal Church in the United States. Two features of its contemporary and historical life stand out. One is its relative difficulty in finding a flourishing place for Aboriginals in its life. Their vernacular culture was largely ignored or eradicated: citizenship was only extended to them in 1967, and the fiction that the land was unoccupied before the first settlement of 1788 remained official history until the late twentieth century.[14] James Noble was the first Aboriginal to be ordained deacon in 1925, but it was not until the 1970s that there were further ordinations. Arthur Malcolm became the first Aboriginal bishop in 1985. In 1988, Archbishop John Grindrod apologized to the Aboriginal and Torres Strait Islanders people for the injustices done to them.

The second feature that stands out is the way patterns of Irish and Scottish immigration to Australia have carried with them particular antagonisms and commitments. Most obviously, the diocese of Sydney has been well-known throughout the Anglican Communion for over fifty years because of its profoundly conservative and outspoken Reformed stance, theologically and socially, which is largely a legacy of Irish Protestantism. This stance has given Sydney diocese more formidable resources to withstand the rapid secularization of Australia and to adapt to charismatic influences.

By contrast, the relationship of the "Anglican Church in Aotearoa, New Zealand, and Polynesia" (its official name) with its indigenous Maori people has been somewhat less tortured, as its name indicates. The initial mission was to the Maori population rather than to the settlers, and a treaty safeguarding the Maori was signed in 1840. This treaty, while inadequately framed and implemented, has nonetheless proved a boon to the indigenous population. The first Maori bishop, F. A. Bennett, was appointed in 1928. Today the church, numbering half a million, maintains the right of every member to choose the cultural stream—Aotearoan (Maori), Pakeha (white), or Polynesian—in which they wish to express their faith. The primacy is accordingly shared between three archbishops, and the 1989 Prayer Book is an intentional celebration of diversity.

Addressing diversity and a complex historical legacy is also the key to understanding the Anglican Church in Canada, which numbers around two million, around half of whom are in Ontario. As in Australia, Canadian Anglicanism took on a strong Irish Protestant character from the nineteenth century, and maintained a prominent role for lay women in mission. Indigenous peoples had often been seen as key military and

13. Ward, *History of Global Anglicanism,* 274.

14. Ward, *History of Global Anglicanism,* 282.

economic allies in the revolutionary period, but later came to be politically marginalized. Anglican missions bore fruit, however, and today a quarter of all First Nations peoples and 85 percent of Inuits are Anglican, comprising a tenth of the Anglican Church in Canada's membership as a whole. However, the systematic stripping away of local culture that took place in the residential schools continues to overshadow this history, and the offering of adequate compensation threatens to bankrupt more than one Canadian diocese, beginning with Cariboo in British Columbia in 2001. Anglicanism has not taken deep root among Francophone Canadians, although the more recent influx of Haitian and Congolese Anglicans has altered this historic tendency somewhat. Canada has led the Anglican Communion in moves toward same-sex blessings, with less (internally) divisive results than corresponding developments in the United States.

The church in Haiti holds a unique place in Caribbean history, postcolonial imagination, and the contemporary Episcopal Church. After a slave revolution in 1804, it became the first independent black-led republic in the world and today it is the poorest country in the Americas. In 1864 James Theodore Holly, an Episcopal priest from Connecticut, brought one hundred of his parishioners there and became the first Anglican bishop of the Haitian Apostolic Orthodox Church in 1874. In 1875 it formally joined the Episcopal Church and is now the church's largest diocese. The cathedral in Port-au-Prince has been destroyed six times, most recently in the Léogâne earthquake of January 2010, which left between 15 and 20 percent of Haitians homeless. The response of the wider Episcopal Church to the plight of its largest but most disadvantaged diocese has been a significant test of the church's desire to enter a postpaternalistic era.

The global efforts from the Church Missionary Society (CMS), the Society (later, the United Society) for the Propagation of the Gospel (USPG), and other English-based organizations have been marked by the prominence of Irish and Scots missionaries. The CMS in particular flourished far more in the nineteenth-century Irish church than it did in the Church of England. While small in number, the Scottish Episcopal Church (50,000), the Church of Ireland (350,000), and the Church in Wales (75,000) have each in different ways modeled a nonestablished Anglicanism.

In Wales, the Reformation affirmed Welsh identity by bringing about the translation into Welsh of the Prayer Book in 1567 and the Bible in 1588. Much later the leaders of the eighteenth-century Welsh Great Awakening were in many cases Anglicans. However, as in England, the established church was unable or unwilling to keep the surge of faith within its structures. As late as 1905, the Church in Wales was still the largest denomination in the principality, and, even after disestablishment in 1922, and perhaps uniquely among Anglican churches, it retains a nonestablished mission to all who dwell in the country.

The 1707 Union with England affirmed Presbyterianism as the established Church of Scotland. Because of its association with Jacobite pretenders to the throne (the last of whom died in 1792), Scottish Episcopalians remained largely in the shadows, indeed sometimes persecuted, until the nineteenth century. Thereafter the church retained a certain social cachet. Presbyterians were said to believe "that the Episcopal Church is an English exotic brought in by the laird [lord] with his background of an English [private] school, or by the laird's English wife, and supported mainly by people who hope the laird will ask them to dinner"—an impression that was strengthened by the invariable appointment of Englishmen as bishops until the later twentieth century.[15] The assertion of a more authentic Scottish tradition, generally Anglo-Catholic in character, and always more deeply rooted in the northeast, was assisted by the publication of Scottish prayer books in 1929 and 1982.

The political manipulation that has often characterized Anglicanism has surfaced perhaps more often, and with greater ill effect, in Ireland than in any other land. Despite the establishment of Trinity College, Dublin, in 1591 to train men for the cause, the Protestant faith did not take hold in Ireland, nor did it help that evangelists assumed that converts should speak English. In the late sixteenth and early seventeenth centuries, English and Scottish Protestants were planted in Ulster and Munster, and 40 percent of the land transferred to their ownership. One outcome was the 1641 rebellion, during which many Protestants were massacred in Ulster. Protestant ascendancy took hold decisively after the defeat of James II by William of Orange at the Battle of the Boyne in 1690. The Act of Union (1801) and the Evangelical Revival encouraged the (Anglican) Church of Ireland in the false hope of making Ireland Protestant. Disestablishment, which came in 1867, was a more realistic statement that religion, like land, needed to be detached from the Irish question as systematically and urgently as possible. After partition in 1922, the Orange Order, a Protestant fraternal organization, continued to hope for Protestant ascendancy in Northern Ireland, while the Church of Ireland remained in many places deeply invested in securing Protestant dominance, although its leadership has been increasingly associated with peacemaking. In the Republic of Ireland, the Church of Ireland continues to be linked to more affluent, influential parts of society, but is much more comfortable with a minority social context.

Conclusion

What does this story of English, American, and global Anglicanism add to the more theoretical chapters that have preceded it? How does the faith

15. Agnes Muir MacKenzie, 1943, quoted in Ward, *History of Global Anglicanism,* 30.

of the Episcopal Church as experienced in practice illuminate, challenge, or enrich its faith as set out earlier in this broad overview? Let us briefly review the earlier claims through the lens of these historical narratives.

Faith is first about the Triune God revealed in Jesus. While sometimes obscured by cultural assumptions or institutional sclerosis, this central claim is as undisputed today as at any time in the history of the Episcopal Church. Perhaps only in the late eighteenth century, when some clergy in England, the United States, and elsewhere had come to suppose preaching was largely about edifying wisdom and civilizing ethics, has this central tenet ever been in serious jeopardy.

Faith is also about the Jews. This has been easier to forget. At times, both the Episcopal Church and the Church of England have come to assume their own nation has taken on the mantle of Israel, displaying some kind of manifest destiny. At other times, anti-Semitism has lurked overtly or covertly, and the Jewishness of Jesus and the historicity of salvation have been obscured. But remembering and being in relationship with the Jews is about being mindful of the faithfulness of God.

Faith is about the Holy Spirit and the church. There is no doubt that the shape of the church—its bishops and sacraments, its worship and mission—has been a preoccupation of the Episcopal Church and has often been the form that focus on the incarnation has taken in new lands. This has also led to a widespread involvement in ecumenical dialogue, not always with the assumption that Episcopalians should naturally chair the meeting. But in recent decades the charismatic experience of the Holy Spirit has become a highly significant aspect of Episcopal spirituality, and throughout its history, times of revival have continued to stretch Episcopal identity and challenge its inclusiveness and flexibility.

Faith is, finally, about salvation. While much of the attention in recent years concerning the church in Africa has fallen on conservative understandings of sexuality, perhaps the most significant question the African churches habitually ask of the rest of the Communion is, "How much of your idea of salvation is realized today?" The emphasis on healing, on signs of God's living power, and on daily dependence on God's providence, are much more in evidence in the African churches, and many would say that is a sign that salvation is real and that the kingdom is close at hand. It is surely part of the crisis of the Episcopal Church, as well as other western churches, that it finds it so hard to express what salvation specifically means today—and even what salvation means eternally—in language reflecting the imagination of the New Testament. Here, perhaps more than anywhere, is where the churches of the Anglican Communion need each other. As they have always done.

BIBLIOGRAPHY

Primary Sources (by chapter)

Chapter 1

Bell, G. K. A. *Christian Unity: The Anglican Position*. Olaus Petri Lectures at Upsala University, October 1946. London: Hodder and Stoughton, 1948.

Church of England. *The Mystery of Salvation: The Story of God's Gift: A Report*. Harrisburg, PA: Morehouse, 1995.

Farrer, Austin Marsden. *Saving Belief: A Discussion of Essentials*. London: Hodder & Staughton, 1964.

Gladstone, William. *Church Principles Considered in Their Results*. London: J. Murray, Hatchard, 1840.

Gore, Charles. *The Incarnation of the Son of God: Being the Bampton Lectures for the Year 1891*. New York: C. Scribner's Sons, 1891.

_____. *Lux Mundi: A Series of Studies in the Religion of the Incarnation*. New York: United States Book Company, 1890.

Greene-McCreight, K. E. "The Only Son of God," in *The Rule of Faith: Scripture, Canon and Creed in a Critical Age*, ed. Ephraim Radner and George Sumner. Harrisburg, PA: Morehouse, 1998.

Jewel, John. *An Apology of the Church of England*. Ithaca, NY: Cornell University Press, 1963.

Levering, Matthew. *Christ's Fulfillment of Torah and Temple: Salvation according to Thomas Aquinas*. Notre Dame: University of Notre Dame Press, 2002.

O'Donovan, Oliver. *The Desire of the Nations: Rediscovering the Roots of Political Theology*. Cambridge: Cambridge University Press, 1996.

Pobee, John S. "An African Anglican's View of Salvation," in *Anglicanism: A Global Communion*, ed. Andrew Wingate, Kevin Ward, Carrie Pemberton, and Wilson Sitshebo. London: Mowbray, 1998.

Quash, Ben. "The Anglican Church as a Polity of Presence," in *Anglicanism: The Answer to Modernity*, ed. Duncan Dormer, Jack McDonald, and Jeremy Caddick. New York: Continuum, 2003.

Ramsey, Michael. *Holy Spirit: A Biblical Study*. London: SPCK, 1977.

Simeon, Charles. *Evangelical Preaching*. Portland, OR: Multnomah Press, 1986.

Stott, John R. W. *Basic Christianity*. Grand Rapids, MI: Eerdmans, 2008.

Tanner, Kathryn. *God and Creation in Christian Theology*. Minneapolis: Fortress Press, 2005.

Taylor, Barbara Brown. *Speaking of Sin: The Lost Language of Salvation*. Cambridge, MA: Cowley, 2000.

Traherne, Thomas, and Denise Inge. *Happiness and Holiness: Thomas Traherne and His Writings*. Canterbury Studies in Spiritual Theology. Norwich: Canterbury Press, 2008.

Wiles, Maurice F. *Faith and the Mystery of God*. Philadelphia: Fortress Press, 1982.

Chapter 2

Butler, Joseph. *The Analogy of Religion*. New York: F. Ungar, 1961.

Dix, Gregory. *The Shape of the Liturgy*. New York: Continuum, 2005.

Hooker, Richard. *Of the Laws of Ecclesiastical Polity*, abridged and ed. A. S. McGrade and Brian Vickers. New York: St. Martin's Press, 1975.

Hoskyns, Edwyn Clement. *The Riddle of the New Testament*, 3rd ed. London: Faber & Faber, 1947.

Ndungane, Njongonkulu. "Scripture: What Is at Issue in Anglicanism Today?" in *Beyond Colonial Anglicanism*, ed. Ian Douglas and Kwok Pui-Lan. New York: Church Publishing, 2001.

Newman, John Henry. *Tracts for the Times*. London: J. G. F. & J. Rivington; Oxford: J. H. Parker, 1840.

Radner, Ephraim. "The Scriptural Community: Authority in Anglicanism," in *The Fate of Communion: The Agony of Anglicanism and the Future of a Global Church*, ed. Ephraim Radner and Philip Turner. Grand Rapids, MI: Eerdmans, 2006.

Robinson, John A. T. *Honest to God*. Philadelphia: Westminster Press, 1963.

Seitz, Christopher. "Creed, Scripture, and 'Historical Jesus,'" in *The Rule of Faith*, ed. Ephraim Radner and George Sumner. Harrisburg, PA: Morehouse, 1998.

Tindal, Matthew. *Christianity as Old as the Creation*. Vol. Faksimile-Neudruck der Ausg, London 1730. Stuttgart-Bad Cannstatt: Frommann-Holzboog, 1967.

Wells, Samuel. *Speaking the Truth: Preaching in a Pluralistic Culture*. Nashville: Abingdon, 2008.

Westcott, Brooke Foss. *The Bible in the Church: A Popular Account of the Collection and Reception of the Holy Scriptures in the Christian Churches*. London: Macmillan and Company, 1913.

Chapter 3

Bolt, Peter. "Interpreting Australian Society for Christian Mission," in *"Wonderful and Confessedly Strange": Australian Essays in Anglican Ecclesiology*, ed. Bruce Norman Kaye, Sarah Macneil, and Heather Thomson. Hindmarsh, S. Aust: ATF Press, 2006.

Chiwanga, Simon E. "Beyond the Monarch/Chief: Reconsidering the Episcopacy in Africa," in *Beyond Colonial Anglicanism*, ed. Ian Douglas and Kwok Pui-Lan. New York: Church Publishing, 2001.

Coakley, Sarah. "Prayer, Place and the Poor," in *Praying for England: Priestly Presence in Contemporary Culture*, ed. Samuel Wells and Sarah Coakley. New York: Continuum, 2008.

Hooker, Richard. *Of the Laws of Ecclesiastical Polity*, abridged and ed. A. S. McGrade and Brian Vickers. New York: St. Martin's Press, 1975.

Jefferts Schori, Katharine. *A Wing and a Prayer: A Message of Faith and Hope*. Harrisburg, PA: Morehouse, 2007.

Jenkins, Timothy. "Anglicanism: The Only Answer to Modernity," in *Anglicanism: The Answer to Modernity*, ed. Duncan Dormer, Jack McDonald, and Jeremy Caddick. New York: Continuum, 2003.

Okorocha, Cyril. "Evangelism in the Anglican Communion," in *Anglicanism: A Global Communion*, ed. Andrew Wingate, Kevin Ward, Carrie Pemberton, and Wilson Sitshebo. London: Mowbray, 1998.

Stringfellow, William. *My People Is the Enemy: An Autobiographical Polemic*. New York: Holt, Rinehart and Winston, 1964.

Thornton, Martin. "The Anglican Spiritual Tradition," in *The Anglican Tradition*, ed. Richard Holloway. Wilton, CT: Morehouse, 1984.

Underhill, Evelyn. *The Mystery of Sacrifice: A Meditation on the Liturgy*. New York: Longmans, Green, 1938.

Venn, Henry. *To Apply the Gospel: Selections from the Writings of Henry Venn*. Grand Rapids: MI: Eerdmans, 1971.

Williams, Rowan. "Being a People: Reflections on the Concept of the 'Laity,'" in *Religion, State & Society* 27, no. 1 (1999): 11–21.

Chapter 4

Chase, Philander. *Reminisces: An Autobiography*. Vol. 1. 2nd ed. Boston: James B. Dow, 1848.

Church of the Province of New Zealand. *A New Zealand Prayer Book*. Auckland: Collins, 1989.

Hassett, Miranda Katherine. *Anglican Communion in Crisis: How Episcopal Dissidents and Their African Allies Are Reshaping Anglicanism*. Princeton: Princeton University Press, 2007.

Hastings, Adrian. *A History of English Christianity 1920–2000*. London: SCM Press, 2001.

Maurice, Frederick Denison, and J. N. Morris. *To Build Christ's Kingdom: F. D. Maurice and His Writings*. Canterbury Studies in Spiritual Theology. Norwich: Canterbury Press, 2007.

Mbiti, John S. *Bible and Theology in African Christianity*. Nairobi: Oxford University Press, 1986.

Prichard, Robert W. "The Place of Doctrine in the Episcopal Church," in *Reclaiming Faith: Essays on Orthodoxy in the Episcopal Church and the Baltimore Declaration*, ed. Ephraim Radner and George R. Sumner. Grand Rapids, MI: Eerdmans, 1993.

Seabury, Samuel, and Anne W. Rowthorn. *Miles to Go before I Sleep: Samuel Seabury's Journal from 1791–1795*. Hartford, CT: Church Missions, 1982.

Selvanayagam, Israel. "Anglicans and Inter-Faith Relations—A Historical Retrospect," in *Anglicanism: A Global Communion*, ed. Andrew Wingate, Kevin Ward, Carrie Pemberton, and Wilson Sitshebo. London: Mowbray, 1998.

Shanks, Andrew. "Honesty," in *Praying for England*, ed. Samuel Wells and Sarah Coakley. New York: Continuum, 2008.

Temple, William. *Christianity and Social Order*. New York: Penguin Books, 1942.

Tutu, Desmond, and John Webster. *Crying in the Wilderness: The Struggle for Justice in South Africa*. 3rd ed. London: Mowbray, 1990.

Vanstone, W. H. *Love's Endeavour, Love's Expense: The Response of Being to the Love of God*. London: Darton, Longman & Todd, 1977.

Ward, Kevin. *A History of Global Anglicanism*. Cambridge: Cambridge University Press, 2006.

White, William. "Case of the Episcopal Churches," in *Readings from the History of the Episcopal Church*, ed. Robert W. Prichard. Wilton, CT: Morehouse-Barlow, 1986.

Wilberforce, William. *Christianity and Politics*. Classics of Christian Statesmanship Monograph Series. Washington, D.C.: Family Research Council, 2004.

Secondary and General Sources

Allchin, A. M. *Participation in God: A Forgotten Strand in Anglican Tradition*. Harrisburg, PA: Morehouse, 1988.

Avis, Paul D. L. *The Anglican Understanding of the Church: An Introduction*. London: S.P.C.K., 2000.

Bartlett, Alan. *A Passionate Balance: The Anglican Tradition*. Traditions of Christian Spirituality. London: Darton Longman & Todd, 2007.

Bernardin, Joseph Buchanan. *An Introduction to the Episcopal Church.* 2nd ed. New York: Morehouse-Gorham, 1955.

Chapman, Mark D. *Anglicanism: A Very Short Introduction.* New York: Oxford University Press, 2006.

Dormor, Duncan J., Jack McDonald, and Jeremy Caddick, eds. *Anglicanism: The Answer to Modernity.* New York: Continuum, 2003.

Elgin, Kathleen. *The Episcopalians: The Protestant Episcopal Church.* The Freedom to Worship Series. New York: D. McKay, 1971.

Greer, Rowan A. *Anglican Approaches to Scripture: From the Reformation to the Present.* New York: Crossroad, 2006.

Griffiss, James E. *The Anglican Vision.* The New Church's Teaching Series. Cambridge, MA: Cowley, 1997.

Hein, David, and Gardiner H. Shattuck Jr. *The Episcopalians.* New York: Church Publishing, 2006.

Holloway, Richard. *The Anglican Tradition.* Mowbray's Christian Studies Series. London: Mowbray, 1984.

Holmes, Urban Tigner. *What Is Anglicanism?* Wilton, CT: Morehouse-Barlow, 1982.

Howe, John W., and Samuel C. Pascoe. *Our Anglican Heritage: Can an Ancient Church Be a Church of the Future?* 2nd ed. Eugene, OR: Cascade Books, 2010.

O'Donovan, Oliver. *On the Thirty Nine Articles: A Conversation with Tudor Christianity.* Published for Latimer House, Oxford. Exeter, England: Paternoster Press, 1986.

Pittenger, W. Norman. *The Episcopalian Way of Life.* Englewood Cliffs, NJ: Prentice-Hall, 1957.

Sykes, Stephen. *The Integrity of Anglicanism.* New York: Seabury Press, 1978.

_____. *Unashamed Anglicanism.* Nashville, TN: Abingdon, 1995.

Williams, Rowan. *Anglican Identities.* Cambridge, MA: Cowley, 2003.

Wilmer, William H. *The Episcopal Manual.* 3rd ed. Baltimore: E. J. Coale, 1829.

STUDY GUIDE

by Sharon Ely Pearson

This study guide is intended to assist the reader in connecting with the text by Samuel Wells as an individual and perhaps part of a small group study. While the book is an introduction to what Episcopalians believe and their roots in the Anglican tradition, it is a view of the "corporate" theology of the Episcopal Church. One of the overarching themes that will permeate this study guide is for you to be able to articulate your own theology, as an Episcopalian or whatever your faith perspective may be.

This guide can serve as an outline for an adult formation class, either in its entirety or in sections. It could easily be a four-week study, each week focusing on a chapter. Or more sessions can be devoted to the text, with four units of study (one per chapter) comprising four to six weeks of study unpacking each of the sections within each chapter. There is much food for thought in these pages, and the reader may find it helpful to be in conversation with others as they explore the faith of Episcopalians, Anglicans, and themselves. Each chapter will offer a means for you to grasp and define concepts presented from the text as well as your own experience and understanding, followed by suggestions for you to explore further on your own to supplement the readings. Lastly, questions are offered to help you delve deeper into your own theology as a Christian, and perhaps an Episcopalian.

I recommended that you keep a personal journal as you read the text, perhaps alongside this guide on a chapter-by-chapter or section-by-section basis. Your journal can also serve as a jumping-off point for small group discussion. In all, my hope is that this guide will be a blending of the two, making Wells's book come alive for you and your beliefs rather than a static set of principles and doctrines that you are looking at from the outside in.

Episcopalians are a "people of the book"—the Book of Common Prayer. Obtain a copy of the 1979 BCP and use it alongside this study guide. Be prepared to open up its pages to read the liturgies, creeds, and historical documents found within it, especially the Thirty-Nine Articles and the Chicago-Lambeth Quadrilateral. Individuals using the Book of Common

Prayer do not usually discover these two documents, but they inform the beliefs of the Episcopal Church, especially in today's world discussion of conformity and unity within the Anglican Communion. Another source to have alongside your study is *The Hymnal 1982*. Much of the Episcopal Church's theology can also be found in its hymns, which this guide will refer to from time to time. The Bible will also be a helpful reference to have on hand.

In his introduction Wells states, "Every generation faces the challenge of bringing these central events face-to-face with the pressing issues of the day, and responding to the questions of the day in ways that are faithful to the manner in which God has already been revealed. Indeed, one may go further and say that, in every generation, God give the church opportunities to rediscover how abundant are the resources of the faith, and how vibrant are the gifts of the Holy Spirit for meeting what would otherwise seem daunting trials." I hope that this study guide, used alongside this book, will help you answer the questions:

- What do Episcopalians believe?
- On what grounds do they (and you) believe it?
- What forms of life emerge from this belief?
- How are these beliefs manifested in the world: past, present, and future?

Chapter 1: The Faith

Introduction: The Triune God; Transformation in Christ

Define:

Belief	Incarnation
Substance	Docetism
Begotten	Neoplatonism
Faith	Resurrection

For further exploration:

- The Chalcedonian Creed of 451 (BCP, 864)
- The Nicene Creed (BCP, 358)
- The Thirty-Nine Articles (BCP, 867)
- An Outline of the Faith (God the Father—BCP, 846; God the Son—BCP, 849; The Holy Spirit—BCP, 852)

Questions for reflection:

1. What is your belief (or nonbelief) of the gender of God? Where do you believe this comes from?
2. For you, what is the heart of your faith?
3. What does it mean to be "begotten"?

4. Make a list and compare and contrast:

   a. How is Christ human?
   b. How is Christ divine?

5. Compare and contrast:

   a. The Nicene Creed
   b. The Thirty-Nine Articles

6. Why is docetism considered a heresy? What do you believe about this concept?

7. Why do you think Jesus' ministry (miracles and teachings) is not referenced in the creeds of the church?

8. Do you believe the Thirty-Nine Articles are important to understand what Episcopalians believe today? If so, why? If not, why not?

9. Why did Jesus allow himself to die?

10. Wells notes three features of Jesus' suffering and death: (1) Jesus' vicarious suffering as a sacrifice; (2) Jesus' nonresistance and forgiving demeanor as he went to his death; and (3) the isolation of Jesus, not just among human beings, but even, perhaps, in the heart of God.

    a. Which ones are you most inclined to agree with or find to live out God's purpose?

    b. Are all of these understandings necessary for what we believe, or if only one or two, which ones (and why)?

11. What do you believe about the concept or existence of hell?

12. How would you describe the resurrection? Do you believe in a spiritual or bodily resurrection? Or both? How do you come to that belief?

13. Wells offers three explanations of Jesus' words to the thief on the cross as what death and resurrection might mean: (1) a promise of immediate entry into heaven upon death for all believers; (2) an unresolved state for all until "the last day" of judgment; (3) there will be a transformation of all forms of life—a new heaven and a new earth—at some time in the future. Which do you believe (if any), and why? Refer to "I Am the Bread of Life" (*The Hymnal 1982*, 335). What viewpoint does this hymn take?

14. Wells states that the understanding that we (humans) must complete the work of Christ is a flawed belief. Why is this? Are there ways that humanity attempts to solve the woes of the world? Turn to the Outline of the Faith (the Catechism) on p. 845 of the Book of Common Prayer. What is the mission of the church? Is this contrary to what the author is stating, or supportive? What do you believe is still to be accomplished, if anything (for us or for Christ)?

The People of God

Define:

Grace	Covenant
Righteousness	Redemption

For further exploration:

- Read Genesis 2:4–3:24 (Adam and Eve) and Genesis 6:5–8:22 (Noah) as well as Genesis 12:1–9 (Abraham)
- Read Exodus 19:1–25, 20:1–17, 20:22–23 (Moses)
- An Outline of the Faith (Old Covenant—BCP, 846) and (New Covenant—BCP, 850)

Questions for reflection:

1. How would you tell the salvation story? What are the important stories to include from Scripture?
2. Why have Christians repeatedly denied Jesus was a Jew?
3. Why is the Old Testament fundamental to the New Testament?
4. How can God redeem humankind through a particular people (the Hebrews) while blessing all people? Why does God bother, if God is God?
5. What is the shift from the Old Testament to the New Testament?
6. How can the church (we) discover the relationship between the Gentiles and the Jews (as God's people)? Is this an important action for Christians to take?

The Holy Spirit and the Church

Define:

God the Father	Salvation
God the Son	Bondage
God the Holy Spirit	Spiritual gifts
Creator	*via media*
Redeemer	Anglican Communion
Sanctifier	Catholic
Apostolic	

For further exploration:

- The Nicene Creed (BCP, 358)
- An Outline of the Faith (The Holy Spirit—BCP, 852) and (The Church—BCP, 854)
- Holy Baptism (BCP, 299) especially p. 306
- 1 Corinthians 12:1–31
- The Baptismal Covenant (BCP, 304)

Questions for reflection:

1. Why is it important to understand the relationship of the Holy Spirit to God and Jesus?

2. Wells states, "What the Holy Spirit does is to overcome the distance of space and time between Christ and the believer, and make Jesus present to the church today" (p. 12). Do you agree? Why or why not?

3. He also explains that the Spirit releases us from bondage (p. 12). Why might this be important to one's faith? How does this occur?

4. What are the characteristics of the Holy Spirit that are different from the characteristics of God or Jesus?

5. Why is the Holy Spirit called upon so prominently in the rite of baptism?

6. Why does the Episcopal Church place more emphasis on some "gifts" than others?

7. What are the visible means in which we see the church and the Spirit interlinked?

8. Is the church necessary?

9. How does the Episcopal Church provide a middle way (*via media*) within the larger Christian community?

10. What does it mean to be both Catholic and Reformed? What's the difference? If you are new to the Episcopal Church, what does this feel like? If you were raised in the Episcopal Church, have you ever thought about this and what does it mean to you?

11. Why is diversity in the body of Christ important? Wells describes the Anglican Communion as the body of Christ. Do you agree? Is the Anglican Communion important? Why or why not? If the Anglican Communion were to cease in it its existence, would that change the beliefs of Episcopalians? Others within the Anglican Communion?

12. If you were accused of being a Christian, would there be enough evidence to convict YOU?

13. What does the word "holy" mean to you? "Holiness"? Wells discusses holiness in terms of "the light of the world" and "the salt of the earth." What is the difference between the two?

14. Name some specific examples of personal spirituality in the Anglican tradition.

15. What is your understanding of "one holy, catholic, and apostolic"?

16. In what ways have churches outside of England found ways to express their catholicity?

17. Has your congregation or diocese partnered with another diocese in the Anglican Communion? What forms does this partnership take? What brought the partnership about? What does it consist of?

18. Would the first apostles recognize your church as living out the faith of the early church?
19. How does your congregation continue in the teaching and fellowship of the apostles?

Creation and the Kingdom

Define:

Creation	Kingdom of God
Grace	Oppression
Will	Injustice
Dispensationalism	Evil
Incarnation	Suffering

For further exploration:

- An Outline of the Faith (Human Nature—BCP, 845) and (The Christian Hope—BCP, 861)
- Read Matthew 13:3–23; 22:1–14 and 25:1–13, 31–16

Questions for reflection:

1. Wells states, "Creation had no necessity but was entirely an act of God's grace. God's will to be in relationship becomes the logic of the universe" (p. 17). How do you interpret this?
2. What does relationship mean to you? How does this connect with God and creation?
3. What is the purpose of creation?
4. Apocalyptic doomsayers permeate the world news today. What is your response to their warnings and predictions?
5. "The world, while it undoubtedly changes significantly as a result of human endeavor, is not fundamentally better or worse than it was a hundred years ago or will be a hundred years from now" (p. 19). Do you agree or disagree?
6. What do you believe the incarnation was?
7. There is much reference to the kingdom of God in Scripture as well as from theologians today. What do you believe the kingdom of God is?
8. Do humans cause suffering?
9. Do humans cause disease or natural disasters, or does God cause them? Both? Neither?

Salvation

Define:

Sin	Sanctification
Salvation	Reconciliation

Justice	Confession
Justification	Redemption

For further exploration:

- An Outline of the Faith (Sin and Redemption—BCP, 848)
- Article IX of the Thirty-Nine Articles (BCP, 869)

Questions for reflection:

1. How do we (humans) bear God's image?
2. How does Jesus exemplify these characteristics?
3. What do you believe is a comprehensive picture of a "flourishing life"?
4. Wells says contemporary Episcopal belief has altered from previous centuries of understandings of what constitutes a "just social order." Do you agree? How have these beliefs changed?
5. Do you believe sin can be eradicated? How? If not, why not?
6. What are the differences and similarities between sin, idolatry, and ingratitude?
7. Wells gives five answers to the question, "How does Jesus save us?" on pages 23–24. Which ones do you agree with most? Least? Why? Which speaks most directly to you?
8. What has been your understanding of what the Reformation was all about? Compare the various doctrines and concepts that developed during this time leading to Methodism, Presbyterianism, Lutheranism, and Anglicanism from the Roman Catholic Church.
9. What is one's vocation? How might you discern your own vocation?
10. Describe your understanding of heaven and hell. Wells describes heaven as "a state of restored, renewed, and fulfilled relationship with God and one another" (p. 27). What would this be like for you?
11. Is Jesus necessary for salvation?

Chapter 2: The Sources of the Faith

Introduction: Revelation and Authority

Define:

Revelation	Natural theology
Revealed theology	Reason
Scripture	Experience
Tradition	

For further exploration:

- Psalm 78
- Hebrews 11

Questions for reflection:

1. What has been your understanding of revelation?
2. What tangible signs of the divine do you see in the world today?
3. Wells introduces the characteristically Episcopal threefold formula of "Scripture, tradition, and reason." Do you believe "experience" should be part of this three-legged stool, or not?
4. How have you seen Scripture, tradition, reason, and/or experience in dialogue with one another as a community discerns the revelation of God?
5. "Without Scripture, it is not possible to know the heart of God, to meet the incarnate Jesus" (p. 32). Do you agree or disagree?
6. How do you believe revelation takes place?
7. Have you ever experienced God through (1) dramatic divine intervention; (2) an embodied devotion; (3) retrospection; (4) full disclosure?

Scripture

Define:

Apocrypha	Source criticism
Old Testament	Redaction criticism
New Testament	Literary criticism
Inspiration	Empirical tradition
Textual criticism	Pragmatic tradition

For further exploration:

- Article IV and Article VI of the Thirty-Nine Articles (BCP, 868)
- A sampling of Apocryphal books: Tobit, Judith, Wisdom of Solomon, Ecclesiasticus (Sirach), Baruch, Susanna, 1 & 2 Maccabees

Questions for reflection:

1. What was the criteria used for choosing the books we find today in the Old and New Testaments? If you were to choose what writings should be part of Holy Scripture, what criteria would you choose?
2. Why do you think the books of the Apocrypha have not been considered canonical by most Protestant traditions, but have been recognized in the Episcopal Church?
3. How is the Old Testament the gospel?
4. How would you describe the God of the Old Testament? What reasons do you have for these descriptions? How would you describe the God of the New Testament? Are they similar, different, or the same?
5. What do you believe the Bible to be?
6. Wells states, "Every reading of Scripture is an act of interpretation that requires attention to earlier readings (tradition) and of the

wider discernment of the church (reason)" (p. 34). What is your understanding of what makes Scripture holy?

7. "All scripture is inspired by God and is useful for teaching, for reproof, for correction, and for training in righteousness, so that everyone who belongs to God may be proficient, equipped for every good work" (2 Timothy 3:16–17). Which view of Scripture do you adhere to most: (1) inspired by the Holy Spirit; (2) inspired by the words themselves; or (3) local inspiration in the life of a community that seeks to embody the text? Do you agree with the passage quoted above from 2 Timothy? Why or why not?

8. Do you believe "Holy Scripture containeth all things necessary to salvation" (the "sufficiency" of Scripture as stated in the Thirty-Nine Articles as well as the Chicago-Lambeth Quadrilateral)? Why or why not?

Tradition

Define:

Tradition
Creed
Council

For further exploration:

- The Apostles' Creed (BCP, 96)
- *Te Deum laudamus* (BCP, 95) and *Gloria in excelsis* (BCP, 94)
- The Lord's Prayer (BCP, 97)
- The Seven Ecumenical Councils: http://www.pbcc.org/dc/creeds/councils.html
  - Nicaea (325)
  - Constantinople (381)
  - Ephesus (431)
  - Chalcedon (451)
  - The Second Council of Constantinople (553)
  - The Third Council of Constantinople (680)
  - The Second Council of Nicaea (787)
- Readings from some of the church "Fathers": http://www.ccel.org/fathers.html
  - Apostolic Fathers: Clement of Rome, Ignatious of Antioch, Polycarp
  - Eastern Fathers: Irenaeus, Origen, Clement of Alexandria, Athanasius, Basil of Caesarea, Gregory of Nazianzus, Gregory of Nyssa
  - Western Fathers: Tertullian, Ambrose, Augustine of Hippo, Gregory the Great

- The Oxford Movement: http://justus.anglican.org/resources/bio/ 249. html

Questions for reflection:

1. What traditions have been handed down in your family? Are any of them religious traditions?
2. Do you have a "Rule of Faith"? What might it look like if you were to create one?
3. Contemporary theologian Jaroslav Pelikan is quoted (in 1984) as describing tradition as not "the dead faith of the living," but "the living faith of the dead." (See the footnote on p. 42 for the full quotation.) How do you interpret this statement for us today?
4. In recent years, tradition has also taken on a "nuanced appreciation for local discernment." This has lead to the focus of passionate disagreement among Christians on topics such as slavery, the role of women, and human sexuality. What issues has the Episcopal Church discerned on the local level that has put it in conflict with the other members of the Anglican Communion?

Reason

Define:

Reason	Theoretical reason
Deductive reasoning	Practical reason
Inductive reasoning	Hermeneutic of suspicion

For further exploration:

- Platonic philosophy: http://www.platonic-philosophy.org/
- Aristotle's philosophy: http://www.aristotle-philosophy.com/

Questions for reflection:

1. What do you believe to be a healthy relationship between Scripture, tradition, and reason? Unhealthy?
2. Name some portions of Scripture or tradition that are based on deductive and inductive reasoning. How could the debate between faith and inductive reasoning be fruitful?
3. What is the difference (if any) between theoretical and practical reason and truth and goodness?
4. Explore Wells's comment regarding challenges to the Christian faith from an Episcopal perspective. "The overall tendency in the Episcopal Church has been to see practical and theoretical reasoning on a continuum. It does not rule out theoretical reasoning as speculative,

or as contrary to Scripture and tradition, but always seek principally
to establish how the truths of theoretical reason may be translated
into the realities of practical existence. Perhaps the most significant
way in which this emphasis is expressed is in assuming the primacy
of worship as the place in which doctrine (or theoretical reason)
is visualized and ethics (or practical reason) is portrayed" (p. 47).
What does this statement mean to you in practical terms?
5. Why is community so important to the Christian faith?
6. How and when can conflict be healthy when understanding one's
   faith?
7. Why has authority always been disputed in the Episcopal Church
   (according to Wells)?
8. How is "reason" a form of prayer?

Chapter 3: The Order of the Faith

Introduction: Holiness; Worship

Define:

Holiness	Sacrament
Worship	Baptism
Ministry	Eucharist
Mission	Liturgy

For further exploration:

- Holy Baptism (BCP, 299) and Holy Eucharist (BCP, 323/355)
- An Outline of the Faith (Sacraments, Holy Baptism, The Holy Eu-
  charist, Other Sacramental Rites—BCP, 857–61)
- Morning (BCP, 37/75) and Evening Prayer (BCP, 61/115)
- An Order for Compline (BCP, 127)
- The Celebration and Blessing of a Marriage (BCP, 423)
- The Burial of the Dead (BCP, 469/491)
- Daily Devotions for Individuals and Families (BCP, 137)
- *The Prayer Book Guide to Christian Education, 3rd edition* (More-
  house Publishing, 2009) offers explanations of the church seasons
  and calendar: http://www.prayerbookguide.com

Questions for reflection:

1. Reread Wells's definitions of worship, ministry, and mission on
   page 50. Do you agree with these explanations? Is anything missing?
   What would you correct, add, or subtract (if anything)? Develop
   your own full definition of each of these interconnected words.

2. The Episcopal Church focuses its identity in a pattern of prayer. How is this different from other Protestant traditions?

3. Why is baptism so foundational to Episcopalians? What does it symbolically and actually represent?

4. As Paul says in Colossians 3:12, we clothe ourselves "with compassion, kindness, humility, meekness, and patience." How do we do this individually, as members of a church community, and as the church itself?

5. Review a service of the Holy Eucharist in the Book of Common Prayer (Rite I, 323 or Rite II, 355). Discern the five movements outlined by Wells in the service. You can also use a worship bulletin outlining the service from your congregation.

   a. Procession and gathering
   b. God's word
   c. People's response
   d. Sharing of food
   e. Sending out

6. What do you believe is the purpose of the sermon?

7. Why is money included in the offering of bread and wine?

8. How are we "to transform sorrow and pain into thanksgiving" in the world as we are blessed and dismissed following Eucharist?

9. What do you believe occurs at the Words of Institution ("This is my body. . . . This is my blood") at the Eucharist?

10. The concept of marriage is much discussed in the world today. What do you believe is the purpose of marriage?

11. How might you begin a practice of daily devotions?

Ministry

Define:

Ministry	Vocation
Ordination	Priest
Deacon	Bishop

For further exploration:

- An Outline of the Faith (The Ministry—BCP, 855)
- Association for Episcopal Deacons: http://www.diakonoi.org/
- Ordination services (Bishop—BCP, 512, Priest—BCP, 525, Deacon—BCP, 537)

Questions for reflection:

1. In An Outline of the Faith, it states, "The ministers of the Church are lay persons, bishops, priests, and deacons" (BCP, 855). Why are lay persons mentioned here—and mentioned first?

2. What do you believe ministry in daily life consists of?
3. What is the difference between vocation and occupation?
4. Do you believe deacons should have a permanent role in the church today? Have you ever experienced the ministry of a vocational deacon?
5. Why are priests ordained deacons before being ordained to the priesthood? Do you believe this is necessary?
6. What do you believe is the role of a priest? Do you agree with Wells's descriptions (intermediary between God and the people as well as between the people and God)?
7. What does a clerical collar represent to you?
8. Who is your bishop? How is he/she the guardian and teacher of the faith of the apostles? What do you believe their role should be in your congregation, diocese, and the world?
9. Review the ordination services for a bishop, priest, and deacon. How are they similar? Different?
10. Why does Wells focus this section on "Ministry" on the ordained orders of ministry? Is there a place for the ministry of all the baptized in this section? What would you have added, if anything?

Mission

Define:

Evangelism	Forgiveness
Mission	Reconciliation
Memory	Injustice

For further exploration:

- An Outline of the Faith (The Church—BCP, 854–55)
- Matthew 25:31–46

Questions for reflection:

1. According to Wells, the work of mission is "to search for lost coins in the household of history, coins that, gathered together, may furnish the present and future with limitless gold" (p. 63). Do you agree with this analogy? What have been the church's "lost coins" in its ministry?
2. When does the mission and unity of the church overlap?
3. The Catechism (BCP, 855) states "the mission of the Church is to restore all people to unity with God and each other in Christ." What do you believe is the mission of the church?
4. Reflect upon the "social ills" (injustices) in the world today. How does your church engage with the community in the mission field at its doorstep? How do you engage in mission?

5. How can an individual (or an institution like the church) forge peace between humanity and the wider creation? What is our responsibility, if any?

Chapter 4: The Character of the Faith

Introduction: Incarnation

Define:

Incarnation

Questions for reflection:

1. Why does Wells believe the incarnation is perhaps the theological term most associated with the Episcopal Church? Do you agree? Why or why not?
2. How is the Episcopal Church different in its Anglicanism from the English Church of its "birth"?

English Legacies

Define:

Parish	Anglicanism
The Book of Common Prayer	Archbishop of Canterbury

For further exploration:

- An Anglican Timeline: http://justus.anglican.org/resources/timeline/
- Thomas Cranmer: http://satucket.com/lectionary/Latimer_Ridley_Cranmer.htm
- Church Missionary Society: http://www.cms-uk.org/

Questions for reflection:

1. Is there a common thread to be found in all the events and dates that Wells reviews in this portion of the book (i.e., Synod of Whitby, Pope Gregory VII, Thomas Cranmer)? Can any of these themes be found in recent history or today?
2. In the past, one parish = one priest. How does this remain the same today? Different? What changes do you foresee in the future?
3. What makes the Book of Common Prayer such a radical concept (in the past and for today)?
4. According to Wells, Anglicanism is about liturgical, doctrinal, and historical commitments. Do you agree? Has an understanding of Anglicanism changed over time? If so, how?
5. Where is the Church Missionary Society active today?

6. As this book is being published, there is great debate and study of a proposed Anglican Covenant. Read the Covenant as well as its accompanying study guide "in the spotlight" on the official website of the Anglican Communion: http://www.anglicancommunion .org/. What are your thoughts on how the Episcopal Church should respond?

7. How do you understand Wells's comment, "Believing is clearly not identical to or even fundamentally characteristic of belonging" (p. 72). Does this ring true for you? What is the difference between the two?

8. Why do you think evangelicals make up the most vibrant, most engaged, and most populous dimension of the Church of England today? Can a similar comparison be made for the Episcopal Church?

American Dreams

Define:

Social gospel
Civil disobedience

For further exploration:

- Social Gospel Movement: http://www.pbs.org/now/society/ socialgospel.html
- The Baptismal Covenant: (BCP, p 304)(http://www.anglican communion.org/

Questions for reflection:

1. Why was the American Revolution seen as a Puritan revolt?
2. Looking back on American history, do you believe the view that excessive authority of bishops still exists today?
3. Do you agree that there should be a separation of church and state? Do you believe this separation exists? If not, where do you see the conflict?
4. How did the Episcopal Church pattern its divisions of governance similarly to the United States government and structure of society?
5. Why did it seem that women (e.g., Pauli Murray, Vida Dutton Scudder) took the initiative in social gospel causes?
6. What is incarnational ministry? Where do you see this at work today?
7. What is the national church ideal? Does this continue today?
8. Explore the tension between the role of the church in civil disobedience and social movements. How is today similar to or different from the 1960s?
9. How is the Episcopal Church polarized today?

10. What does "Will you strive for justice and peace among all people, and respect the dignity of every human being" mean to you?
11. What are your thoughts about the opinions of some that social causes are a distraction from the central call to worship, discipleship, and evangelism in the church today?

Global Dimensions

For further exploration:

- Kairos Document: http://www.sahistory.org.za/article/kairos-document-1985-0
- Society for the Propagation of the Gospel (USPG): http://www.uspg.org.uk/

Questions for discussion:

1. What is the difference between Anglican and Episcopal?
2. What impact and meaning does the growth of Anglicanism in Africa have on the Episcopal Church?
3. What role has the Episcopal Church played in the spread of the gospel in Africa in the past and today? Does your church or diocese have a mission partner relationship with an overseas diocese? How is this lived out?
4. How has Anglicanism embraced or marginalized indigenous populations? What can we learn from this?

Conclusion

Questions for discussion:

1. How does the faith of the Episcopal Church as experienced in practice illuminate, challenge, or enrich its theology, worship, spirituality as set out in this book?
2. How would you define "faith" now?

Biography

Sharon Ely Pearson is the Christian Formation Specialist for Church Publishing Incorporated.